D1521209

AMERICAN FOLK MUSIC AND FOLK MUSICIANS SERIES
Edited by Ralph Lee Smith and Ronald D. Cohen

Appalachian Dulcimer Traditions

Ralph Lee Smith

*American Folk Music and
Folk Musicians, No. 2*

The Scarecrow Press, Inc.
Lanham, Md., & London
1997

SCARECROW PRESS, INC.

Published in the United States of America
by Scarecrow Press, Inc.
4720 Boston Way
Lanham, Maryland 20706

British Library Cataloguing in Publication Information Available

Library of Congress Cataloging-in-Publication Data

Smith, Ralph Lee, 1927–
    American dulcimer traditions / Ralph Lee Smith.
        p.   cm. — (American folk music and folk musicians ; no. 2)
    Includes bibliographical references, discographies, and index.
    ISBN 0-8108-3378-6 (cloth : alk. paper)
    1. Appalachian dulcimer—History.   I. Title.   II. Series.
ML1015.A6S63   1997
787.7'4—dc21   97-20990
                                                               CIP
                                                               MN

ISBN 0-8108-3378-6 (cloth : alk. paper)

∞ ™ The paper used in this publication meets the minimum
requirements of American National Standard for Information
Sciences—Permanence of Paper for Printed Library Materials,
ANSI Z39.48–1984.
Manufactured in the United States of America.

To the people of the Southern Appalachian mountains, known and unknown, who developed the dulcimer and preserved its traditions,

and

To my parents, Hugh and Barbara Smith, Pennsylvania rare book and antique dealers, who taught me to love old things.

Contents

Acknowledgments

I write a column on dulcimer history called "Mountain Dulcimer Tales and Traditions," for the quarterly magazine *Dulcimer Players News*. Many readers of the column have contacted me to pass on intriguing leads or to tell me about exciting discoveries. Some of the information and some of the photos that they have provided ended up in my column and from there journeyed to the pages of this book. I am deeply grateful to all of these informants, who share my fascination with dulcimer history.

Most of the information about West Virginia's pioneer dulcimer maker, Charles N. Prichard, that appears in chapter 4 originally appeared in an article in the *Swarthmore College Bulletin*. I wish to thank the *Bulletin* and *Dulcimer Players News* for permission to use material that originally appeared in their pages.

Photos that appear in the book without attribution were taken by the author.

Happy reading!

March 1997
Swarthmore, Pa.

1

An American Heritage

The dulcimer comes to us out of the mists of the Appalachian mountain past. Prior to the post–World War II urban folk revival, its craftsmanship and its musical traditions were centered in the world of the Allegheny, Blue Ridge, and Great Smoky Mountains. Dulcimers were handmade, and the makers of most specimens prior to the twentieth century are unknown.

Beginning in the 1950s, dulcimer making and playing moved into the national mainstream as part of the post–World War II urban folk revival. By the 1970s, interest in the dulcimer's history had begun to grow. By then, most of the history had been lost.

To a unique degree among major folk instruments, unearthing of historical information on the dulcimer cannot be done in museums or libraries. Most surviving old dulcimers are not in museums, and most museums have little information about dulcimers. There is virtually no "paper trail." Such information as we are ever likely to have comes directly from surviving old instruments and from the fading memories of Appalachian old folks.

Most of what has been learned about the dulcimer in the past twenty years reflects the enthusiasm of a small number of persons who have combed the mountain world, made friends who knew where something might perhaps be learned or found, stretched meager assets to buy old dulcimers, and enthusiastically exchanged information with one another in the evening when phone rates are cheap. Much of what this book contains was generated by this happy and busy jungle telegraph.

This book is not a narrative history of the dulcimer. I have written such a book, called *The Story of the Dulcimer*, which readers are invited to consult. The present book focuses on certain major traditions and certain important persons. The following brief overview of the dulcimer's development will help the reader to understand how the persons and traditions described here fit into the dulcimer's overall history.

The Hammered Dulcimer

The word "dulcimer" is used to describe two instruments that are not musically related. No one knows why both instruments have the same name. One is now known as the hammered dulcimer, the modifying adjective added in modern times to distinguish it from the dulcimer that is the subject of this book. The hammered dulcimer is a trapezoidal-shaped instrument, with many courses of strings passing over one or two bridges. The strings are struck with hammers that are held in each hand. This type of instrument originated in the Middle East in medieval times and spread to both Europe and China. It was brought to America from Europe during the colonial period. A modern hammered dulcimer is shown in figure 1.1.

Hammered dulcimers were made in small shops in the United States in the nineteenth century, in places that included New York State and Michigan. In the 1890s, the Sears Roebuck Catalog offered hammered dulcimers for $20. However, they fell into relative disuse during the twentieth century and were not rediscovered until the 1970s. Like the type of dulcimer that is the subject of this book, the instrument is enjoying a renaissance today, with skilled makers and players active throughout the United States and with many recordings of hammered dulcimer playing available in virtually every music store.

The King James Version of the Bible mentions the dulcimer twice in the Psalms, and this mention has sometimes been cited as an authority for the antiquity of the Appalachian dulcimer. The confusion is evident in the 1959 newspaper article that is reprinted in appendix D. However, there is a double error. First, the type of dulcimer that is the subject of the reference is the hammered dulcimer, which was well known in Elizabethan England and was obviously known to the King James translators. However, these translators mistranslated the Greek word "symphonia" as "dulcimer." A symphonia is actually a form of bagpipe.

As with the hammered dulcimer, the type of dulcimer that is the subject of this book did not acquire a modifying adjective until the folk revival, when awareness of the fact that two different types of instruments had the same name began to spread. Choosing the adjective proved to be difficult and contentious. The instrument is variously known today as the Appalachian dulcimer, the mountain dulcimer, the fretted dulcimer, and the lap dulcimer.

Only the adjective "fretted," which is a physical description, fits the instrument in the same exact way as the adjective "hammered" fits the other type of dulcimer. As a subjective matter, I do not find the term "fretted dulcimer" appealing, and I don't think that the old folks would care for it very much. Since the type of instrument to which this book is devoted is fully clear, I will do for the balance of the book what was always done in the past—just call the instrument a dulcimer, without an adjective.

In its traditional world, the instrument's name was and is widely pronounced "dulcymore" or "delcymore." In Ohio it has been known by the beautiful name "dulcerine." In West Virginia, where the mountaineers have their own approach to many things, dulcimers were sometimes called "hog fiddles." Perhaps West Virginia hogs can play them!

Early Development of the Dulcimer

Curiously, the dulcimer's ancestry does not trace back to the British Isles, where no instrument like it has been found. Research in recent years has established that the dulcimer is the American member of a family of northern European folk zithers. The Germanic member of this family of instruments is called the *scheitholz* in German and the *scheitholt* in English. Other European instruments that belong to the family include the Swedish and Danish *humle*, the Norwegian *langeleik*, the Icelandic *langspil*, the *hommel* or *nordische balk* of the Low Countries, and the French *epinette des Vosges*. Interestingly, no member of this instrument family is traditional to the British Isles, the ancestral homeland of the people who developed the dulcimer from the scheitholt in America. Scheitholts were made in America by early German settlers. They followed German migration down the Great Wagon Road that ran from Philadelphia through the Valley of Virginia, westward with the western fork of the road beginning at present-day Roanoke, and yet farther west by way of the Wilderness Road, which extended the long trail into Kentucky. The history of this diaspora, with maps and with illustrations of instruments, is summarized in my book *The Story of the Dulcimer.*

Many scheitholts have been found in the area of Pennsylvania known as the Pennsylvania Dutch country. Chapter 2 describes and illustrates a scheitholt made in Pennsylvania in 1788. Specimens have also been found throughout Appalachia, reflecting German settlement in the region. Scheitholts were made and played in Appalachia as late as the twentieth century, although the tradition died out in the Pennsylvania Dutch country before 1900.

Scheitholts both resemble and differ from dulcimers. The similarities and differences are described in chapter 2. Exactly when and how the differences emerged is not known. No frontier of our dulcimer knowledge is more interesting than this one. Three things are clear, however:

1. Scholars agree that the dulcimer developed as a modification of the scheitholt. The reasons for their certainty about this are set forth in chapter 2.
2. Among old dulcimers that have thus far been found, the oldest one of certain date has an inscription that reads as follows: "Floyd County Virginia made by John Scales Jr August the 28th 1832."[1]
3. A number of instruments have been found that appear to be a "reaching out" from traditional scheitholt design, although they do not fully resemble dulcimers. Perhaps—and it's a big perhaps—one or more of these instruments represent the transition from scheitholt to dulcimer design. One such type of instrument is shown and described in chapter 2.

If John Scales was not the first dulcimer maker and if the instrument dated 1832 is not the first dulcimer, it seems reasonable to guess that the earliest dulcimers date back to within a few years before or after 1800.

The Traditional Period

The dulcimer's traditional period extends from the beginnings to about 1950. During this entire period, dulcimer making and dulcimer playing remained largely a regional tradition in Appalachia.

In the earliest type of dulcimer, the body might be described as "boat shaped"; that is, it has only a single wide point. John Scales's 1832 dulcimer is of this design, and Virginia is the principal home of this tradition. Such instruments, virtually uninfluenced by the urban folk revival, are made in southwestern Virginia today. Instruments of the Virginia tradition, and a Virginia family that has been making them for more than 100 years, are described in chapter 3.

Sometime after the Civil War, dulcimers of "hourglass" shape, with upper and lower wide points separated by a waist, began to appear. Chapter 4 describes some old-time makers of this type from West Virginia and North Carolina, and chapter 5 describes the Cumberland mountain tradition in Kentucky.

During its traditional period, the dulcimer was principally a solo instrument. Its place was generally in the home. It often stood in a corner or was placed over a fireplace mantel, where it was correctly regarded as a fine decoration. The fact that it was usually not played with other instruments in its traditional world is strongly indicated by the history of commercial "hillbilly" and "country" recording during the 1920s, 1930s, and 1940s. Thousands of string band recordings were made during this period, but the author knows of none in which the instrumentation included a dulcimer.

Reflecting the dulcimer's role as a "home instrument," many old time players were women. Whether they were men or women, few traditional dulcimer players could read music; they played by ear rather than from musical score. Some players accompanied themselves with singing, while others were content just to play tunes.

Our knowledge of living players indicates that the repertoire of traditional players ranged from material that was exclusively of folk origins, to a mixture of folk tunes and tunes whose composers are known. Jacob Ray Melton, a member of Virginia's foremost dulcimer-making and dulcimer-playing family described in chapter 3, plays traditional tunes only and does not accompany himself with singing. Mrs. Hassie Hicks Martin of Hindman, Kentucky, provided me with a list of songs that she could recall her sister Corinne playing on a dulcimer made by the old-time maker James Edward Thomas, which was given to Corinne by their father in 1924: The Wearing of the Green, Old Man River, Nellie Gray, Danny Boy, The Little Mohee, The Ship That Never Returned, Wildwood Flower, Barbara Allen, Corinna Corinna, and, says Hassie, "special religious songs." Corinne sang with her instrument.

Musical Features of the Dulcimer

The dulcimer's musical features differ in a number of ways from those of other stringed folk instruments in common use in America.

First, unlike other fretted instruments such as the guitar, banjo, and mandolin, the dulcimer is not fretted in a regular progression of halftones. Instead, it is fretted in a pattern of whole tones and halftones, which enable it to play musical scales without the intervention of any tones that do not belong to the scale. This type of fretting is called "diatonic." To provide a more familiar example, the scale of a standard harmonica is also diatonic. If the harmonica is in the key of C, the harmonica simply plays the C major scale: C, D, E, F, G, A, B, C. It doesn't play the intervening halftones that are provided by the piano's black keys.

By contrast, the fretting of an instrument such as a guitar provides all of the twelve tones running from C to C that include both the white keys and the black keys of the piano. This type of fretting is called chromatic.

The scales that the dulcimer will play are not necessarily tied to any particular key. Instead, they are the scales of the ancient musical modes. Each musical mode consists of a series of seven tones, of which five are whole tones and two are halftones. The eighth tone completes the scale at the octave. The modal scales are differentiated from one another by the different places at which the two halftones enter the eight-note progression.

The scale that we call the major scale is one of these modal scales. In ancient times it was called the Ionian mode. If one plays the major scale in the key of C on the piano—that is, C, D, E, F, G, A, B, C—one sees that there is no intervening black key (halftone) between E and F and between B and C. The musical pattern of the scale is therefore whole tone, whole tone, half-tone (no black key between E and F), whole tone, whole tone, whole tone, half-tone (no black key between B and C).

Transferring this pattern to the dulcimer's fret board, one finds that, if one begins a scale at the third fret and advances fret by fret down the fretboard, picking the string at each fret, one has played the major scale. The two halftones, represented by the two short spaces between frets, intervene at the correct places.

Note that, although we are using the white keys of the piano in the key of C to illustrate the major scale, the scale thus played on the dulcimer is not necessarily in the key of C. The actual key is a function of the pitch to which the strings are tuned.

The names of the seven musical modes, the places where they lie along the white keys of the piano, and the places where they lie along the dulcimer fret board, are as follows:

Ionian (major)	C to C	3rd to 10th Fret
Dorian	D to D	4th to 11th Fret
Phrygian	E to E	5th to 12th Fret
Lydian	F to F	6th to 13th Fret
Mixolydian	G to G	Open String to 7th Fret
Aeolian (melodic minor)	A to A	1st to 8th Fret
Locrian	B to B	2nd to 9th Fret

Of the seven modes, Locrian is unknown in American folk music, and Phrygian and Lydian are rare. Ionian is of course common, with Dorian, Mixolydian, and Aeolian all being represented by a significant number of tunes.

At least some old-time dulcimer players understood their instrument's capability for playing scales other than the major (Ionian) scale. Traditional Virginia dulcimer players played on both their Ionian and Mixolydian scales, and some Kentucky players may have used the Dorian and/or Aeolian scales for such tunes as ''Pretty Polly.''

Some 80 percent of all American folk tunes lie along one or another of the pure modal scales, and can be played with perfect accuracy on the dulcimer. Many modern tunes are more sophisticated, and require chromatic fretting to play them correctly. This was of little concern to the old-time player, who played such tunes ''as close as I can, with what I've got!''

Old-Time Playing Techniques

Since the dulcimer was not usually played with other instruments, the traditional player was usually not concerned with the exact key to which the strings were tuned. A good tension of the strings was all that was wanted. We know today that ''good tension'' generally means that the first note of the major scale lies somewhere between the keys of C to E, although an old-time Virginia dulcimer with a short string span can easily be brought up to F.

In the most common dulcimer tuning, the bass string, which is the string farthest from the player as the instrument sits on the lap or on a table, is brought up to a satisfactory tension, and the other two, of thinner gauge, are tuned in unison five tones higher. If the bass string were tuned to C, this would mean CGG; if D, then DAA, and so forth. In old times, a banjo second string was often used for the bass, and banjo fourth strings were often used for the middle and melody strings. Today sets of dulcimer strings with precise gauges are available.

If the strings were tuned CGG, then the melody string—the one closest to the player—when fretted at the third fret, would produce C an octave higher than the bass string, producing the chord C'-G-C. Starting there and running from the third to the tenth fret, the player can play the major (Ionian) scale on the melody string. Additional notes lie above and below the basic octave. Playing in other modes requires starting the scale at a different place and retuning one or more strings.

In the traditional playing method, the player depressed the melody string with his or her finger, a stick, or some small object such as a piece of goose quill, and lined out the melody on this string only. The strings were struck with a finger, a feather, or some type of flexible pick. Single strokes were used for slow songs, rhythmic back-and-forth strokes for more rapid tunes. The two unfretted strings produced a two-tone drone beneath the melody. Occasional traditional players picked the three strings individually to produce patterns of individual notes, but this was not the usual method.

The frets of traditional dulcimers were often made of broom wire, a thin, flexible type of wire that could be bought in rolls at the local general store and used for making brooms. Alternatives were standard shop wire or fence wire. The frets were bent into the shape of staples and inserted into the fret board.

By modern standards, old-time dulcimer fret placement was often approximate, sometimes producing intervals so audibly "off" as to distress the modern listener. There is no indication, however, that the problem bothered the traditional player.

The maker was careful to ensure that the frets extended under the melody string, which was to be fretted, but he was often careless as to whether the frets extended fully under the bass string, which was not fretted. In old-time Kentucky dulcimers, "short fretting" is systematic. Instruments made by such Kentucky makers as James Edward Thomas and Jethro Amburgey have short frets extending fully under the melody string only. The middle string, instead of being equidistant between the melody and bass, has been moved close to the bass, providing a closely paired drone that is away from the frets. This can be seen on instruments by these makers that are illustrated in chapter 5.

The Dulcimer and the Urban Folk Revival

Beginning about 1950, knowledge of the dulcimer spread rapidly beyond Appalachia as part of the urban folk revival. Making and playing of dulcimers were disseminated throughout the country by happy enthusiasts who had no direct relationship to Appalachian traditions. Makers with high levels of skill produced instruments of great beauty and musical quality, with designs and shapes that were often original rather than continuations of older traditions. Today, prices of finely crafted modern instruments can exceed $2,000, in contrast to the $5 or so that dulcimer makers typically charged prior to World War II.

The dulcimer's musical features and capabilities were also expanded. A change with great impact was the use of standard modern musical frets instead of wire bent into the shape of staples. With modern fretting that extended fully across the fret board came the capability for chording all three strings. This, in turn, fostered playing methods in which individual strings were plucked.

Next, additional frets were laid into the fret board to increase playing flexibility. The addition of a fret between the sixth and seventh frets of the traditional scale—the so-called $6^1/_2$ fret—was common by 1960, and is nearly universal today unless the buyer tells the maker that he or she doesn't want it. A $1^1/_2$ fret is also becoming common.

The consequences of these changes can be heard at all present-day dulcimer workshops and gatherings. At a session of the Annual Dulcimer Playing Workshop at Appalachian State University, one class learned to play Pachelbel's *Canon* in five parts. Instructors at many workshops play and teach classical music, blues, ragtime, and jazz. All of this is done on an instrument whose capabilities hardly extended beyond "Sourwood Mountain" a few decades earlier.

In Appalachia, a generation of makers who had begun by making dulcimers in the traditional way in the 1930s, 1940s, and 1950s were swept into the revival. They adopted modern fretting, adopted the $6^1/_2$ fret, secured scientifically measured fretting patterns, and participated in the market that the revival had created. However, many of them retained traditional designs and patterns for their instruments. They brought the old world into the new. Four Appalachian makers of the folk revival transition are described in chapter 6.

The reader will note from this overview that the book's coverage does not extend to the most recent chapter of the tale—that is, to modern, non-Appalachian dulcimer makers and dulcimer making. This is a great subject, but requires a book of its own. My book is devoted to the old-time dulcimer, from its earliest beginnings to the great Appalachian makers of the folk revival transition, who are now gone or growing old.

Library of Congress Dulcimer Recordings

The earliest commercial recordings of the dulcimer are products of the post–World War II folk revival. However, the Archive of

Folk Culture of the Library of Congress contains a number of field recordings of the dulcimer, extending back to 1934. The earliest dulcimer recordings in the Archive are these four:

287–308 Twenty-two 12-inch disks recorded at the American Folk Song Festival, Jean Thomas, director, in Ashland, Kentucky, June 1934.
    291 A   "The Pateroller Song." Sung with dulcimer by Uncle Tom West.
    302 A1 "Ground Hog." Sung with dulcimer by Curtis Dartley.
    302 A2 "Turnip Greens." Same as above.
    302 B   "Barbara Allen." Same as above.

Other Library of Congress dulcimer recordings are listed in this book, at the end of the chapters to which they apply.

The Library of Congress will provide taped copies of any of the recordings listed in this book, for use by individuals for research and/or for learning songs and tunes. Fees are moderate. Recordings supplied in this fashion cannot be used for commercial purposes. To secure taped copies of songs, send a letter or fax to the Archive of Folk Culture, Library of Congress, Washington, DC 20540-8100, fax (202) 707-2076, providing the following information:

- The songs or tunes that you wish to receive. The citations in this book will enable Archive personnel to identify what you want.
- A statement of the purpose for which you wish to use the material.
- Whether you wish to receive the material in reel-to-reel or cassette format.

The Archive will respond by sending you a sheet of instructions and an order sheet. Fill out the order sheet and send it in. The Archive will review your request and will notify you of the cost of filling your request. If you have additional questions, call the Archive at (202) 707-5510.

Note

1. L. Allen Smith, *A Catalogue of Pre-Revival Appalachian Dulcimers* (Columbia: University of Missouri Press, 1983), 46–47.

Figure 1.1   A modern hammered dulcimer. Courtesy Sam Rizzetta.

2

✚

Dulcimer Ancestors and Cousins

The scheitholt that was disseminated by the early German migration was a straight-sided instrument, usually with vertical iron tuning pins, and with its set of frets applied directly to the edge of the body that faces the player. Some two hundred years ago, or perhaps more, this instrument passed across cultures on the early Appalachian frontier and was modified by early Scotch-Irish and English settlers. It emerged as an instrument with angular or curved sides, with horizontal tuning pins made of wood, and with frets placed on a raised and centered fret board. That is, it emerged as a dulcimer. Exactly what happened, and when, and where, cannot now be known, although it is possible to do some educated guessing. We will do some in this chapter.

Scheitholts and dulcimers are both *diatonically fretted zithers*. Each of the three words is important.

- The instruments are *zithers* because, in formal musical terminology, a zither is any instrument in which the strings extend over the body without a neck.
- Not all zithers are *fretted,* but scheitholts and dulcimers are both fretted instruments. An additional feature that most traditional specimens of both instruments share is that they have at least one string that does not pass over the frets and is not intended to be fretted.

13

- Scheitholts and dulcimers are both *diatonic*. As is explained in chapter 1, this means that their fret patterns consist of a series of whole tones interspersed at certain intervals with halftones, arranged in such a fashion that the instruments play scales without intervening halftones or accidentals. With most scheitholts and most dulcimers, the first tone of the "major" scale is at the third fret. Less commonly in scheitholts and quite uncommonly in dulcimers, the "major" scale begins at the open string.

This chapter describes a fine scheitholt, two types of instruments that are related to the scheitholt, and a unique instrument that was patented in the 1930s.

Samuel Ache and His Scheitholt

The instrument that is illustrated in figure 2.1 is one of the finest American scheitholts that has yet been discovered. As an added wonderful touch, the Pennsylvania German inscription running along its side indicates that it was a gift of love from the maker, Samuel Ache, to his fiancée.

The instrument is owned by Jeanette Hamner of Hampton, Virginia. It passed down in her mother's family, who come from the Lancaster area of Pennsylvania. In the early 1990s, Jeanette and her husband Charles, now deceased, brought it to Ken Hamblen, a well-known dulcimer maker of Salem, Virginia, for restoration.

Early in 1993, I called Ken to check on an old dulcimer that was reported to have passed through his hands. The dulcimer, it turned out, had been brought to him for restoration by an intermediary for an owner who did not wish to deal with outside parties. I agreed with Ken that we should not disturb this person. But Ken had some other interesting news.

"The dulcimer was one of two instruments that I have recently restored," he said. "The other was an old scheitholt that was signed and dated, and had a long inscription in Pennsylvania Dutch running along its side. I think the date was 1788."

At my request, Ken contacted the Hamners to see if they would be willing to talk to me. I quickly received a postcard from Jeanette, giving me their phone number and inviting me to call.

Colonial Williamsburg

On the phone, the Hamners described the instrument to me in detail. As we were talking, an idea came to me. I wonder, I said, if Colonial Williamsburg, which is not far from Hampton, might like to see the instrument. The Hamners gave me permission to call and find out.

I called Colonial Williamsburg and talked to Martha Katz-Hyman, an assistant curator. Yes, Martha said, they would very much like to see it. I called the Hamners back, and they personally delivered the scheitholt to Colonial Williamsburg for study.

Colonial Williamsburg specialists examined the instrument and prepared a three-page Curator's Work Sheet. The work sheet includes a detailed description of the instrument, and the full text of the Pennsylvania German inscription, with an English translation.

Features of the Scheitholt

The work sheet states that the scheitholt is made of maple and a softwood, perhaps pine. It has nine strings, of which three pass over fourteen frets and the others are grouped in pairs of two. Note names inscribed between the frets show two octaves of the scale in the key of C, with C, at the open string, not having a stenciled letter. The stenciled letters are D, E, F, G, A, H, C. Following ancient German nomenclature, "H" is used instead of "B" for the seventh tone of the scale.

The sound holes, the work sheet states, consist of three sets of round holes, "two of which form squares (a center hole with four perimeter perforations that go through the belly and four that do not) and one of which forms a cross (with one center perforation that goes through the belly and four that do not), all of which are defined by concentric scribe lines."

The basic color of the instrument is an old orange-red, with the exception of the bottom, which is unfinished. The decoration, the work sheet says, consists of "painted and inked decoration in black and red on all surfaces except the bottom, which is unfinished. Decoration on belly includes wavy lines with circles as a border and around sound holes, stylized flowers, vines and scrolls . . . on tuning head penned ink scallops and free-form scrolls and leaves on top and sides; on long side, stylized tulips, scrolls, vines and flowers (similar to *fraktur* decoration); on short side, inscription penned in black ink between scribe lines with inked decorative letters and other decoration."

The inscription, translated into English, reads as follows: "This heart of mine shall be given to you alone, amen it will come true, we will sing and play an entire [wood abraded and word or words missing; perhaps lifetime?] Hendelberg Township, Dauphin County, 27 February Samuel Ache 1788." (See figure 2.2)

How Was It Tuned and Played?

As noted, this scheitholt has three strings passing over the frets, and six others arranged in pairs of two. In stringing the instrument, Ken Hamblen tuned all of the three strings that pass over the frets, to the same note, C.

Ken surmised that the three pairs of strings passing to the right of the frets were intended to provide accompanying harmony notes for each of the three basic chords—tonic, subdominant, and dominant—in the tonic key. He therefore tuned these strings to produce two tones for each of these three chords in the key of C.

From this set of tunings, a likely playing method emerges. The player lined out the melody on the three identically tuned strings that pass over the frets. Harmonies could be produced by plucking the appropriate pair of strings to the right of the frets at intervals that suited the player. If this is correct, it suggests that the strings of this instrument were picked with the right hand rather than bowed.

The fretting of this scheitholt raises some interesting questions, which are discussed in appendix B.

A Speculation Becomes Reality

In the mid 1970s, Ph.D. candidate L. Allen Smith spent more than a year crisscrossing the Appalachians in an old van, searching for and photographing old scheitholts and dulcimers. He located thirty-seven scheitholts and 155 dulcimers made prior to 1940. He summarized his findings in a Ph.D. thesis and in a book entitled *A Catalogue of Pre-Revival Appalachian Dulcimers*, published by the University of Missouri Press in 1983.

Looking at instrument after instrument in the course of his monumental fieldwork, Smith formulated a question. Suppose one took a long, narrow scheitholt and placed a sound box beneath it. The scheitholt would lose its independent identity, and would become the head and fret board of the larger instrument that was thereby created. Wouldn't this new instrument be a dulcimer? The answer was, perhaps so, but the beast remained mythical. Smith hadn't found one, and neither had anyone else.

That was the state of events until Josie Wiseman attended a local auction near her home in Pewee Valley, Kentucky, on a summer day in 1986. Josie had been a student in my dulcimer history class at the annual Dulcimer Players Workshop at Appalachian State University in Boone, North Carolina, and she knew of Allen Smith's speculations about the "scheitholt mounted on a sound box." She therefore knew exactly what she was looking at when she saw a strange musical instrument among the items being offered for sale. Another person bid against her and raised the price to more than Josie wanted to pay, but he was wasting his time. Josie rushed home with her prize and called me.

"Ralph," she said breathlessly, "I've found one!"

"What did you find?" I asked.

"A scheitholt mounted on top of a sound box!"

I was nearly speechless. I finally said, "Where is it?"

"It's here!" she cried. "I bought it at an auction. It's mine!"

Josie's find is shown in figure 2.3.

A Remarkable Photograph

A totally unexpected additional chapter was added to this tale in 1992, when I visited Ken Kurtz, a college classmate who lives in Lexington, Kentucky, in connection with my search for information on "Uncle Ed" Thomas, the old-time Kentucky dulcimer maker who is discussed in chapter 5. At the Lexington Public Library, Ken showed me an old photograph of a dulcimer player that appears on page 243 of a book entitled *Our Kentucky: A Study of the Bluegrass State*, edited by James C. Klotter, and is reprinted in figure 2.4. The caption read, "The dulcimer is a mainstay of folk music."

I made a copy of the photo without really looking at it, but when I examined it later I gasped. The dulcimer on the player's lap appears to be a virtual duplicate of the one found by Josie, or may even be the identical instrument!

A credit line that accompanies the photo in the book states that it was provided by the Kentucky Historical Society. I called the society. They checked their records and found that the man in the picture is named F. M. Waits, that the picture was taken in Frankfort, Kentucky, in 1929, and that it is one of a number of photos taken by a now-defunct photo studio that found their way into the society's collection. That is all that anyone knows.

Allen Smith's Latest Thinking

Meanwhile, Allen Smith continues to reflect. A summary of his most recent thinking appears in a 1993 publication called *Blue Ridge Folk Instruments and Their Makers*. This was issued in connection with an exhibition of dulcimers and other instruments that was mounted by the Blue Ridge Institute in Ferrum, Virginia.

In essence, Allen states that he is now less inclined to assume that the dulcimer evolved through a number of transitional steps such as a ''scheitholt mounted on a sound box.'' The dulcimer as we know it could have been created directly, in a single step, without any transition. There is no question that this could be so. If you like mysteries, you will love this one. Look at the pictures here and ponder.

Scheitholts-in-Boxes

Scheitholts-in-boxes are rare American folk instruments. In my ''Dulcimer Tales and Traditions'' column in the July–September 1993 issue of *Dulcimer Players News,* I described the only three specimens that were known at that time. Readers promptly contacted me to tell me about three more. The three described in my article are as follows:

- Figure 2.5 shows a specimen found and purchased by Randolph M. Case of Lawrenceville, Georgia.
- Figure 2.6 shows a specimen owned by Don Koerber of Warren, Michigan. Two other pictures of this instrument appear on pages 45 and 46 of my book *The Story of the Dulcimer*.
- A third instrument was illustrated in the ''Queries'' column of *Antiques* Magazine, January 1932. The photograph is reproduced on page 32 of L. Allen Smith's *Catalogue of Pre-Revival Appalachian Dulcimers*.

All three specimens have a hinged lid. Opening the lid reveals a raised portion shaped like a long right triangle, with head and tuning pins at the truncated apex, which is set into the rectangular top surface of the box.

The First One Discovered

The photo in the January 1932 issue of *Antiques* was submitted by a reader identified only as "W. L. W." The instrument has six strings, of which two pass over the frets. The top and the inside of the lid are stencil-painted with charming designs, including sailboats and five rocking horses, one of which appears beneath the strumming area. In publishing the picture, the magazine said, "The character of the stenciling points to a date somewhere in the first quarter of the 1800s."

Mr. R. P. Hummel, the authority to whom *Antiques* submitted the query, replied with impressive accuracy that the instrument "appears to be an elaboration of the primitive zither which was popular among the Pennsylvania Germans in the eighteenth century, and of which several are preserved in the Mercer Museum of Doylestown, Pennsylvania." The Mercer Museum's instruments are scheitholts. All seven that are owned by the museum are illustrated in Allen Smith's book, and three of them are shown in mine.

Two More Are Found

When Allen Smith wrote his book, the instrument illustrated in *Antiques* was still the only one known. But when I attended the Great Black Swamp Dulcimer Festival as an instructor in the spring of 1983, Don Koerber, who was at the festival, told me that he had acquired one. Figure 2.6, a front view of the instrument, is one of several photos that Don sent to me. Good views of the box closed, and of the stenciling on the top of the instrument, appear in *The Story of the Dulcimer*.

Don's instrument has a finely shaped, grain-painted box and lid, and stands on small feet. The name "E. BECKWITH" is stenciled on the front of the lid. There is stenciled ornamentation on the top and the inside of the lid, including two lions, an eagle, and the words "Columbian Improved Harp." As with the instrument illustrated in *Antiques*, there are six strings of which two pass over the frets. Letters corresponding to notes of the musical scale are stenciled in the spaces, between the frets, beginning with D.

For eight more years there was no additional news about scheitholts in boxes. Then, at the 1991 Appalachian Dulcimer Workshop at Appalachian State University, Randolph Case, a workshop attendee, told me that one had come into his possession.

As figure 2.5 shows, it is a beauty. It has seven strings of which five pass over fifteen frets. There is no stenciling on the inside of the lid, but the stenciling around the sound holes is finely executed. As with Don Koerber's instrument, notes of the musical scale beginning with D are stenciled along the fret board. The superb craftsmanship includes a well-shaped scheitholt head, undoubtedly made by someone familiar with the scheitholt and its traditions. The tuning pins are unlike any others that I have seen.

Two More Beckwiths

Shortly after the appearance of my column, Lee Vaccaro of Rochester, New York, wrote to me as follows: "I received my *DPN* last midweek, and I was tickled to see your article on the dulcimer-in-a-box, or scheitholts. I've had one around for a year or so, that I bought at a flea market."

Lee's instrument, like Don Koerber's, was made by E. Beckwith. Here is her description:

> Mine is labeled in gold, as you described Don Koerber's, "E. Beckwith Maker" along the front panel of the right triangle, with lovely gold stencilling of red flowers in a pot, and lyres with wings inside the lid, and a wheat stalk down one soundhole, and a stylized daisy and leaves across the other.

As with Don's instrument, six strings pass over fifteen frets. Comparison of the photo with the two photos of Don's instrument in my book shows that the beautiful box, the shape of the sound holes, and the stenciling around the upper sound hole are basically the same in both instruments. However, the stenciling around the lower sound hole and on the inside of the lid are notably different.

Early in 1996, Ray and Lorraine Steiner of Webster, New York, called to tell me that they had acquired a Beckwith. Subsequently they sent me photos and a letter that said in part, "We haven't been able to find much information about it, except that it was purchased originally in New York State by the dealer. The original owners had no information about it." The town of Webster is not far from Rochester, where Lee Vaccaro lives. This suggests the possibility that E. Beckwith made his instruments in New York State, perhaps in Rochester.

News from South Carolina

In February 1994, Mary Kick of Mount Pleasant, South Carolina, called me in a state of great excitement, and she followed up her call with a letter that read in part as follows:

Rella King and I play in a dulcimer group in this area. Also, we receive the *Dulcimer Players News* and read every word you write. A week and a half ago, I loaned her my notebook with all the class handouts and my notes from my week at the Dulcimer Workshop at Appalachian State.

The next day, Rella's neighbor told her of a strange instrument at a local shop. Rella called me, and we met on Monday to see the unusual instrument. As I told you, I think we were both a little disappointed to find the instrument quite so primitive, but we were thrilled at the same time.

After Mary's and my phone conversation, she and Rella teamed together to buy the instrument. Mary and Rella subsequently donated it to the Appalachian Cultural Museum at Appalachian State University. The instrument is illustrated in figure 2.7.

The sound holes closely resemble those of the Beckwith instruments. The top of the "triangle" is made of beautiful tiger maple. A notable difference between this instrument and the other four that are known is the simple decoration, which is confined to handsome and, in fact, stylish stripes that are painted on the top.

The name "Bennett" is stenciled on the bottom of the box, and the initials TLB are scratched in script in the center of the bottom. There is no way to know whether this person was the maker or an owner.

Musical Features

Of the six specimens described here, all except Randolph Case's instrument are fretted in such a fashion as to play the major/Ionian scale from the open fret. This fretting makes it possible to stencil letters in the intervals between the frets that indicate notes of the scale of C Major—C, which is the open string and therefore does not have a stenciled letter, followed by the stenciled letters D, E, F, G, A, B, C. This procedure was followed by "E. Beckwith."

Randolph Case's instrument presents the same anomaly as the Ache scheitholt (see appendix B). Lettering for the C Major scale, beginning with D, is stenciled along the fret board as described above. However, the instrument is fretted in the same fashion as a traditional dulcimer, so that the major/Ionian scale begins at the third fret. The seventh note of the scale from the open fret is therefore really B flat, not B as is stenciled on the fret board. These instruments were almost certainly intended for use by the general public. One wonders what the owners thought when they reached the seventh note of the scale!

A Folk Craft Frontier

Virtually nothing is yet known about scheitholts-in-boxes other than the physical evidence of the instruments themselves.

- The triangular-shaped instrument body that is shared by the instruments thus far discovered indicates that they have a common prototype.
- At one time, the basic design was known to a number of craftspersons.
- The quality of the workmanship and the ornamentation of all the instruments makes it virtually certain that they were made in small shops and were intended for commercial sale.

Perhaps the original idea, and some of the instruments, emanated from the shop of a skilled German-American zither maker as a relatively simple, easy-to-play variant on his main line of products. But that's guesswork. As with so many features of dulcimer history, we have barely started down this path of discovery.

A Fretted Zither With Foot Pedals

In October 1995, Kay Zingsheim, a *Dulcimer Players News* reader in Overland, Kansas, sent me several pictures of a remarkable instrument. In her letter, Kay said in part:

> I play hammered dulcimer and am in the Prairie Dulcimer Club. At our June 2nd Festival, a man from southern Missouri walked into the festival carrying this dulcimer on his shoulder, and informed everyone that he wanted to get "rid of this thing, it's been taking up space in my storage shed for 25 years." I looked it over with some of my fellow club members and paid the man what he was asking.

The instrument (figure 2.8) is made of walnut and is thirty-seven inches long, fifteen inches wide, and twenty-seven inches high. The eleven pedals, all in operating condition, control eleven stops that depress five strings running over a series of frets. A sixth string runs over a separate set of frets that duplicate the intervals of the frets under the fivestring set for the first eleven frets, and continues beyond for another octave. The intervals of the fret sequence are chromatic. The stops make it possible to play barre chords to accompany a melody played on the sixth string.

The label on the front panel reads "SIEGRIST Dulcimer PATENTED." Kay did some research and made a fascinating discovery. In 1878, a person named Paul L. Siegrist, who lived in New York State, received a patent for a loom that was operated by dampers.

Further checking revealed that the fall 1980 issue of *Dulcimer Players News* carried a letter and accompanying photograph from a reader named Joe Williams of Hoyt, Kansas. The instrument in Joe's photograph strongly resembles Kay's instrument, complete with eleven stops and foot pedals, except that its body is shaped like a large hourglass-style dulcimer. "The only thing we know about it," Joe wrote, "is that it was made by a chiropractor in Plainville, Kansas about 50 years ago."

Another important piece of evidence appeared in the April 1981 issue of *Frets* magazine. Writing in the magazine's column, "Experts Corner," Michael Rugg states that he had seen Joe Williams's letter and photo in *Dulcimer Players News*, and was adding to the historical record the patent drawing for the Siegrist dulcimer (figure 2.9). As soon as this item was called to my attention,

I called the Patent Office and ordered a copy of the drawing and accompanying application. The application and the drawing, which is reproduced in figure 2.10, shows that Charles C. Siegrist applied for the patent on August 10, 1933, and that the patent was granted on January 15, 1935.

"This invention," Siegrist says in the application, "relates to musical instruments and particularly musical instruments on the order of dulcimers." The invention, he says, provides a "means whereby an instrument of this character may have certain of its strings fretted or stopped by a finger [Siegrist's word for a stop] operated by the foot of the player to thus provide for the sounding of a chord . . . the melody may be played by the performer on one string and the chords by the performer on the remaining strings under the control of the fingers [stops]."

The patented version has the dulcimer-shaped body of the instrument shown in the photo that accompanies Joe Williams's letter in *Dulcimer Players News*. As patented, the instrument had only three stops, whose placement suggests that they were meant to play subdominant, dominant, and tonic chords as desired to accompany the melody—analogous to simple three-chord guitar playing.

Siegrist foresaw that he might improve and modify his invention as he went along. "While I have illustrated one embodiment of my invention," he wrote, "I do not wish to be limited thereto, as it is obvious that many changes and variations might be made in the instrument without departing from the spirit thereof as defined in the appended claims."

One would like to know a lot more. Was there a family relationship between Paul Siegrist, the inventor of a type of pedal loom, and Charles Siegrist, the inventor of a "pedal dulcimer"? Did Charles Siegrist bring the dulcimer to Kansas, which is not its traditional world, and, if so, from where? Did he sell many of his instruments, to which he devoted so much time, effort, and cabinetmaking skill? What did they cost?

One thing is certain. Charles Siegrist showed once again what the dulcimer has shown throughout its history—that its possibilities intrigue people and constantly stimulate new ideas, new approaches, and inventions.

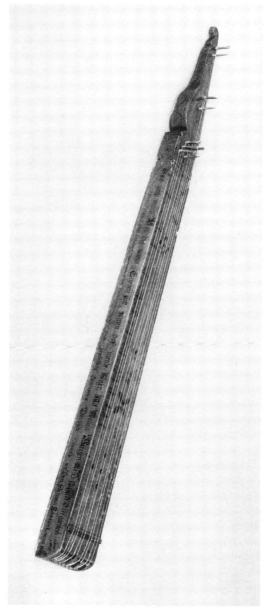

Figure 2.1   The Samuel Ache 1788 scheitholt. Colonial Williamsburg Foundation. Used with permission.

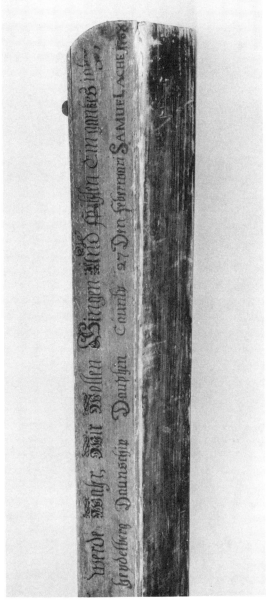

Figure 2.2   Portion of the inscription, showing location, date, and Samuel Ache's name. Colonial Williamsburg Foundation. Used with permission.

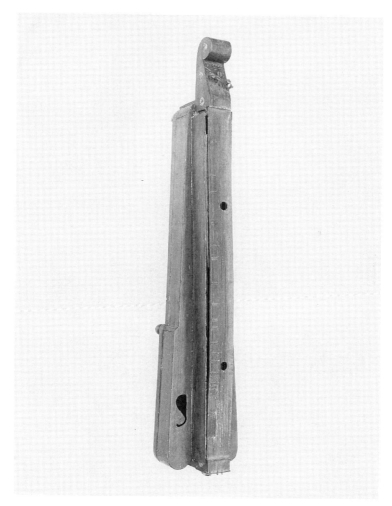

Figure 2.3 *Josie Wiseman's "scheitholt on a sound box."* Gary Putnam.

Figure 2.4 F. S. Waits of Frankfort, Kentucky, holding a dulcimer that strongly resembles the instrument purchased at auction by Josie Wiseman. Kentucky Historical Society.

Figure 2.5   Randolph M. Case's scheitholt-in-a-box opened. Randolph M. Case.

Figure 2.6   Don Koerber's scheitholt-in-a-box opened. Don Koerber.

Figure 2.7 Scheitholt-in-a-box purchased by Rella King and Mary Kick, and donated by them to the Appalachian Cultural Museum. Appalachian Cultural Museum.

Figure 2.8 The Siegrist dulcimer. Lisa Zingsheim.

Figure 2.9   Detail of Siegrist dulcimer, showing the stops extending over five strings, and a second set of frets passing under a sixth string. The sixth string is missing. Lisa Zingsheim.

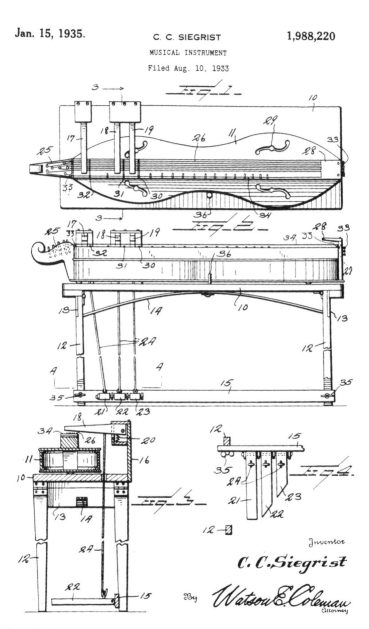

Figure 2.10   Patent drawing of the Siegrist dulcimer.

3

The Dulcimer in Virginia and the Melton Family

In June 1993 I attended the Annual Dulcimer Playing Workshop at Appalachian State University as an instructor in dulcimer history. I invited Jacob Ray Melton, an old-time Virginia dulcimer maker and player, to come with me to the workshop, to explain old-time traditions, to sell his dulcimers, and to perform.

On the stage at the workshop concert, sixty-nine-year-old Jacob Ray (figure 3.1) performed in public for the first time. He placed one of his big double-bottom dulcimers on his lap, removed a stripped turkey quill from his shirt pocket, and played "Ebenezer," a tune that his sister Ruth had played to win the dulcimer contest at the Old Fiddler's Convention in Galax, Virginia, in October 1935, and "Walkin' in My Sleep," which his mother, Lina Whittington Melton, had played to win second place. He received a standing ovation.

The Melton family of southwestern Virginia has been making and playing dulcimers for more than a hundred years. This family is our most direct link to the old and early history of the dulcimer. We will begin by reviewing the major features of the Virginia dulcimer tradition and will then look at the work and heritage of the Meltons.

Features of Old-Time Virginia Dulcimers

Sometime during the first half of the nineteenth century, a type of dulcimer emerged in southwestern Virginia that probably represents the oldest dulcimer tradition. After the scheitholt, and perhaps after certain transitional instruments, comes the Virginia style. We can see its basic features in a fine dulcimer owned by a lady named Polly Sumner, of Pulaski, Virginia, which is illustrated in figures 3.2, 3.3, and 3.4. Polly loaned the instrument to the Jeff Matthews Memorial Museum in Galax, where I saw and photographed it.

All that Polly knows of the instrument is that it has been in her barn for a very long time. The maker is unknown, but he or she was a fine country craftsman and folk artist. The instrument came with a bow, which is not unusual for nineteenth-century Virginia dulcimers.

The body does not have the hourglass shape of the instruments made by Charles N. Prichard of West Virginia and James Edward Thomas of Bath, Kentucky, nineteenth-century makers whose work is described in succeeding chapters. Although the popular image of the dulcimer is of an hourglass-shaped instrument, the hourglass shape probably evolved after 1850, and was never adopted in traditional times in Virginia. The sides of old Virginia instruments move out to a single wide point, like Polly's. Most are curved, although a smaller number are diamond-shaped or lozenge-shaped. The top and bottom of Polly's instrument slightly overlap the sides, a design feature that is not easy for a country craftsperson to execute, but is nevertheless often seen on both Virginia and hourglass instruments.

This instrument has four equidistant strings, reflecting a major Virginia tradition. By contrast, old hourglass-shaped instruments have three strings. A piece appears to be broken off the head. Perhaps it wrapped around in a small scroll. The pegs appear to be old, well-executed replacements.

The frets of Polly's dulcimer consist of pieces of wire bent into the shape of staples and inserted into the fretboard. These frets pass under only two of the four strings. If current Virginia playing styles reflect old traditions, as they almost certainly do, all four of the strings on Polly's dulcimer would have been tuned to the same note. The player would have fretted the two that pass over the frets with a stick or piece of goose quill, leaving the other two to sound as drones.

Although the popular image of a dulcimer is an instrument with heart-shaped sound holes, old Virginia dulcimers never have them. The sound holes are either S-shaped or consist of various patterns of small drilled holes, or of diamonds. In Polly's instrument, the upper pair of sound holes consists of a pattern of small diamonds, and the lower pair consists of small holes in an S-shaped pattern.

A feature that Polly's dulcimer shares with most old Virginia instruments is the presence of two or more sound holes that are drilled into the fret board. The fret board is hollowed out, and, with the holes, becomes in effect part of the sound box. Drilled fret boards are not found on old hourglass-shaped dulcimers, although the fret boards are sometimes hollowed out.

Old Virginia dulcimers do not have a depression or "strum hollow" at the foot of the fretboard, to provide clearance for the action of the strummer. Such a depression is a standard feature of old hourglass-shaped dulcimers and represents a sensible improvement on the Virginia pattern. Its absence in Virginia dulcimers results in damage to the bottom of the fret board by the strummer. Such damage, consisting of grooves worn in the wood, can be seen in Polly's instrument. Most old Virginia instruments show plenty of strumming damage, and in a few cases the wood has been worn all the way through.

Polly's instrument had three small feet, a feature that it shares with many old dulcimers of both the Virginia and hourglass traditions. A pattern of sound holes is drilled into the bottom, a feature that is common in old Virginia instruments but does not appear in hourglass dulcimers.

Virginia dulcimers often have semicircular tailpieces, either solid, pierced with one to three holes, or open in the shape of the letter D. Polly's dulcimer has an open-D tailpiece with a horizontal strut in the middle of the D. The outer surface of the D is handsomely beveled, as is the outer surface of the head.

A final feature worth noting is the vibrating string length, called the VSL, of the strings from the nut (upper bridge) to the bridge (lower bridge). The VSL of Polly's dulcimer is 25^1/$_4$ inches, which falls within the usual 24- to 26-inch VSL of most traditional Virginia dulcimers. By contrast, the VSL of most traditional hourglass-shaped dulcimers is 28 to 29 inches.

This difference affects the range of comfortable tension of the strings, with the comfortable tuning range of old Virginia-style dulcimers running one or two keys higher than that of old-time hourglass dulcimers. In modern times, the shorter VSL of old Virginia dulcimers has been largely abandoned.

The Patriarch: Stephen B. Melton (1817–1897)

The progenitor of the Melton family was Stephen B. Melton, who was born in 1817. In 1836, he married Elizabeth Bryant, who was also born in 1817. She bore him ten children, and died in 1884. As mountain men often did, when the wife who bore him a large number of children died, Stephen married a much younger woman, Caroline E. Todd, born in 1850. Caroline died in 1918, 101 years after her husband was born.

No one knows whether Stephen was involved with the dulcimer. In view of subsequent family history, it seems likely that he was, but we have no instruments or other record of it. What is clear is that we are dealing with dulcimers by the time that we come to two of Stephen's sons, Amon (1840–1925) and Stephen (1852–1917). If this Stephen had a middle name or initial, I could not discover it. We will call him Stephen II to avoid confusion with his father.

Amon Melton (1840–1925)

The existence of a dulcimer that was owned by Amon Melton and may have been made by him was unknown until I got a tip while I was in southwestern Virginia in the summer of 1993. Go to Harmon's Western Wear, outside of Hillsville, I was told. The owner, G. H. "Gooch" Harmon, is a mountain history buff who has built a large addition onto his store to house the "Harmon Museum." There are a couple of dulcimers in there, people said.

I entered Harmon's and asked if I could see the museum. Gooch smiled broadly and waved toward the wide entrance on the opposite wall. Inside the museum, I found myself wandering through an awesome assortment of mountain artifacts, from Indian arrowheads to original copies of newspapers describing murderous mayhem that occurred in the Hillsville courthouse in 1912. No visitor to southwestern Virginia should miss this wonderful private museum.

In a dusty corner with some old farm tools, there were two large diamond-shaped dulcimers, one made by Jacob Melton and one made by Raymond Melton, both of whom we will soon discuss. Jacob's may have been made in the 1930s, Raymond's in the 1960s. They are fine specimens, but I knew where to find other dulcimers made by these brothers. I was looking for something older, and I found it, in two steps.

Hanging on the wall was the first document I had ever seen that related to Jacob and Raymond's grandfather Amon. It was a certificate to operate a legal still. The certificate is an Internal Revenue Service form dated September 15, 1879, entitled *Report of Survey of Stills Used for Distilling Brandy From Apples, Peaches, or Grapes, Exclusively*. The form provides detailed information on the features and capacity of a copper still located on "Steve Melton's Plantation" in Woodlawn, Carroll County, and owned by Amon. The form says that the still was capable of producing 7.8 gallons of apple or peach brandy in 24 hours.

This form harks back to days long before the income tax, when a major portion of U.S. revenue was raised by the taxation of alcohol and tobacco. The Revenue Service maintained a large network of locally based persons in the mountains, who monitored every kind of distilling apparatus for the purpose of collecting tax. In those days, Uncle Sam had no problem about home brew as long as the tax was paid.

One of the veteran employees at Harmon's is Virgil Melton. Virgil's father, Glenn, was a first cousin to Jacob and Raymond. Virgil doesn't make dulcimers, but when he and Gooch learned about my interests, they told me that Virgil's uncle, Rodney Melton, owns a very old dulcimer that had belonged to Amon. As far as Virgil and Gooch knew, no folklorist had ever seen it.

The next day Virgil brought it in, and figure 3.5 shows him holding it. This important instrument appears to represent a link between the mainstream of the Virginia style and certain characteristics that became prominent in Melton family dulcimers.

The instrument is diamond-shaped. The diamond theme appears in the upper sound holes of Polly's dulcimer and turns up frequently in both the body design and the sound hole design of dulcimers made by various members of the Melton family in the twentieth century. However, dulcimers this old with diamond-shaped bodies are uncommon.

The Smithsonian Institution owns an old diamond-shaped dulcimer, reportedly from North Carolina, that is rounded at the bottom. It is illustrated in Allen Smith's *Catalog of Pre-Revival Appalachian Dulcimers*, page 63. The instrument differs in numerous respects from Amon's dulcimer. Among other things, the absence of holes drilled in the fret board indicates little relationship to the Virginia tradition. My book, *The Story of the Dulcimer*, illustrates a diamond-shaped instrument from western North Carolina, page 34, whose sound hole pattern, including two holes drilled in the fret board, exactly duplicates that of Amon's instrument. The instrument shown in my book is otherwise much more archaic than Amon's. I urge readers to compare this instrument with Amon's and make their own guesses.

The top and bottom of Amon's dulcimer overlap its sides. A pattern of sound holes is drilled into the bottom. The instrument is painted red. The semicircular tailpiece is pierced with three large holes. The tailpiece and head are both tapered. The VSL of Amon's instrument is $25^1/_2$ inches (figure 3.6).

Of significant interest is the integration of mechanical tuners into the design of the peg head. Mechanical tuners are sometimes found in old Virginia dulcimers other than those made by the Meltons, but in many cases they appear to be later replacements for wooden pegs. Depressions have been cut into the bottom of the peg head of this dulcimer to accommodate the turning of the tuners, making it certain that the tuners are original with the instrument and integral to its design. In the twentieth century, mechanical tuners became a standard feature of Melton family instruments. Until recently, they were usually cut from plates of guitar or mandolin tuners.

Stephen II (1852–1917)

In 1891, Amon's younger brother, Stephen II, made a dulcimer as a wedding present for Amon's son Samuel (1863–1933) and Samuel's bride, Maggie Todd (1874–1960). This instrument, shown in figure 3.7, has a double bottom, like Jacob Ray Melton's instrument made about a century later, which is illustrated in figure 3.1. The VSL is $25^7/_8$ inches.

The apparent purpose of the double bottom is to keep the sounding bottom off one's lap, and thereby to prevent the vibration of the sounding bottom from being damped. It takes the place of the combination of feet and of sound holes in the bottom, which were designed to provide maximum volume when the instrument was played on a table.

Big-bodied instruments of this type have come to be known as "Galax style" dulcimers. They became widely disseminated in Carroll and Grayson counties in the general vicinity of Galax, which lies on the border between the two counties, during the late nineteenth and the twentieth centuries. It is not known whether Steve Melton, some other Melton, or someone who was not a Melton, originated the style.

The top and bottom of Stephen II's dulcimer overlap its sides. The tailpiece closely resembles that of Amon's instrument, and both tailpieces are tapered. The body, however, is a departure from Amon's instrument. It can be seen as an enlargement of the body style of Polly Sumner's dulcimer, which, in common with many other old Virginia instruments, was already beginning to exhibit significant width and height.

The upper sound holes consist of four small holes that form a diamond—the same pattern as the upper sound holes of Polly's dulcimer, except that the holes are round. The lower sound holes consist of four small holes in an S-shaped pattern. These are common sound hole design themes in old Virginia dulcimers in general and Galax-style dulcimers in particular.

Playing Galax-Style Dulcimers

To play Galax-style dulcimers, the old-time player depresses two of the four strings with a stick or piece of goose quill, allowing the other two to sound as drones. He or she plays with a stripped turkey quill. The carefully cut quill is held by its thicker end, with the thin end to the strings. The use of the long quill permits swifter strumming than is possible if one holds a flexible strummer between index finger and forefinger, which players in other traditions usually do. To hear this instrument, with its great body, swiftly played with a quill, and without a bass sound by consequence of having no bass string, is one of the wonderful experiences of world folk music.

High Tide: Samuel and Maggie's Family

Between 1892 and 1917, Samuel, Amon's son, and his wife, Maggie, had fourteen children. This family produced dulcimer activ-

ity that is unique in American musical history. One virtually
needs a scorecard to keep track.

To begin with, Maggie herself played, using a bow, a skill that
no subsequent family player ever acquired. Three of her boys,
Jacob (1893–1967), Daniel (1905–1977), and Raymond (1915–1985)
made and played dulcimers, with Jacob and Raymond being especially active.

Additional players included Jacob's wife, Lina Whittington
Melton (1893–1957), one of Virginia's outstanding players. Her
sister Myrtle (1901–?), who married Pierce, another of Samuel
and Maggie's children, also played, and so did Pierce and Myrtle's daughter Blanch.

Jacob passed his dulcimer-making and dulcimer-playing skills
to his son, Jacob Ray (1923–), and to his daughter, Ruth, who
married Roscoe Russell. Roscoe also became a fine player, winning the Galax Old Fiddler's Convention competition in 1976.
Roscoe and Ruth's daughter, Bonnie (1960–), won the Galax Fiddlers Convention competition when she was fourteen.

The output of the dulcimer makers in this family is much
smaller than the output of two old-time makers in Kentucky,
James Edward Thomas (1850–1933), who made nearly 1,500 instruments, and Jethro Amburgey (1895–1971), who made about
1,300. Only a few dulcimers were made by Jacob and Daniel prior
to World War II. When Jacob and Lina Melton were interviewed
in connection with their recording session for the Library of Congress in 1937, Lina told John A. Lomax that her husband had
made six dulcimers. He subsequently made a number more. In
an interview that was published in *The Galax Gazette*, August 5,
1981, five years before his death, Raymond said that he had made
dulcimers for his children and had sold about thirty.

Reasons for this difference include the superior access to
Northern markets that was enjoyed by the Kentucky makers because of their association with settlement schools in the mountains of eastern Kentucky (see chapter 5). In addition, Galax-style
dulcimers and dulcimer playing represent far more isolated and
inaccessible musical traditions than dulcimers and dulcimer playing that stemmed from the Kentucky tradition. Even in the folk
revival world of today, only a few aficionados play old-time Virginia dulcimers in the traditional style.

Jacob Melton (1893–1967)

Jacob was a skilled woodworker who worked as a case fitter for a furniture company in Galax. Figure 3.8 shows Jacob in front of his woodworking shop on his property behind his house in Woodlawn, Virginia, in 1966, with two dulcimers and a home-made banjo. The instrument on his lap has a double bottom. The diamond-shaped pattern of round sound holes on the instrument leaning against the shed was the principal sound hole motif for most of Jacob's round-sided, double-bottom instruments. With the instruments made by Jacob, Daniel, and Raymond, the overlap of the top and bottom over the sides, used by Amon and Stephen II, disappears.

It is believed that Jacob showed his two brothers how to make dulcimers. The pattern for his round-sided, double-bottom dulcimers appears to be the instrument made by Stephen II. No one knows where Jacob got the idea and the pattern for diamond-shaped dulcimers, but Amon's dulcimer is a logical suspect.

Daniel Melton (1905–1977)

Daniel, who was a factory worker, made dulcimers that resemble the diamond-shaped instrument made by his brother Raymond that is illustrated in figure 3.9. In 1937, Daniel made a diamond-shaped dulcimer as a wedding gift for Raymond and his bride, Oma Myers. Raymond especially liked this instrument. He used it at prewar Old Fiddlers Conventions in Galax, and for general playing well into the postwar years.

Daniel made a few dulcimers in the postwar period and was a fine player, but maintained a low public profile. His idea of the best place to play was on a front or back porch, with his brothers, family, and friends. Jacob and Raymond participated in the dulcimer competitions at the Galax Old Fiddlers Convention, which Daniel did not do.

Raymond Melton (1915–1985)

Raymond's first job was at a sawmill, where he worked long enough and saved enough money to build the modest house in Woodlawn, near Hillsville, in which he and his wife, Oma, lived. He next worked in a furniture factory in Galax, and at one point left the mountains for about a year to work in a Ford plant in Cleveland. Finally, from 1957 until his retirement in 1972, he worked at the Radford Arsenal.

There is no certain record that Raymond made any dulcimers before World War II. He probably got started in the 1960s, and most of the instruments that survive were probably made after his 1972 retirement. Although still within the old family style, they exhibit great variety and originality.

Figure 3.9 shows the diamond-shaped dulcimer made by Raymond that is in the Harmon Museum. It has a single bottom into which a sound hole has been drilled. Gooch Harmon believes that it dates to the 1960s. Two features are of special interest. First, the instrument has a $6^1/2$ fret, an addition to the dulcimer fret board that was made after World War II by non-Appalachian makers and players of the urban folk revival. Second, the instrument's VSL is $27^1/8$ inches. Raymond has broken with Virginia's ancient twenty-four- to twenty-six-inch VSL tradition, and joined the longer string length of hourglass-shaped dulcimers.

Raymond (figure 3.10) was one of Virginia's and the world's greatest old-time players. In the *Galax Gazette* interview cited above, Raymond said that he had been playing the dulcimer since he was sixteen, which would be about 1931. After the war, he played in local bluegrass bands, made a number of recordings with these groups, and performed at many venues both within and beyond the mountains, including the Newport Folk Festival and the Smithsonian Folklife Festival. He was the terror of dulcimer contests, filling up his living room with ribbons and trophies.

Contest Winners

In spring 1935, the Moose Lodge in Galax, looking for ways to raise money to build a new facility, put on a Fiddler's Convention. The event was successful, and the Moose Lodge promptly scheduled an expanded convention for October 1935. This event was also successful, and the convention has been held annually ever since, except for the war years 1943–1944. Particulars on the dulcimer contests at the convention, from the book *The First Forty Years of the Old Fiddlers Convention, Galax, Virginia*, appear in appendix C.

During the period from 1935 to 1942, the Melton family virtually made the dulcimer contest their private preserve. First-place, second-place, or third-place winners in the period from 1935 to 1942 included: Jacob; Raymond; Lina; Jacob and Lina's daughter Ruth; and Pierce and Myrtle's daughter Blanch. Raymond won first place in 1937, 1939, and 1940. He may have won first place in 1938 too; the records of the 1938 contest have been lost.

John A. and Elizabeth Lomax, the folk song collectors, attended the 1937 convention, and recorded Maggie Todd Melton, Raymond, Jacob, Lina, and Myrtle for the Archive of Folksong of the Library of Congress. The tunes that the Lomaxes recorded are listed in the Library of Congress section at the end of this chapter.

When the convention was resumed after World War II, the dulcimer contest was dropped and was not reinstated until 1974. Of the five winners in 1974, first place went to Bonnie Russell, second place went to Raymond, and fourth place went to Roscoe.

Carrying the record beyond the coverage of the book, Raymond won first place in the dulcimer contest in 1975, playing "Flop Eared Mule," and also won the award for best performer in the entire convention. Roscoe Russell won first place in 1976, playing "Sugar Hill." In 1985, in a large field of contestants that included many players with high sophistication in the revolutionary folk revival playing techniques, Raymond won second place. His ability to win had spanned 48 years. He died less than two months later.

It is interesting to note that another person, Velma Nester Musser, was also a winner in the 1930s and again in the 1970s. Velma won second place in 1937, second place in 1939, and fifth place in 1974. In 1965, several tunes played by Velma Musser were recorded for the Library of Congress; they are listed at the end of the chapter.

Jacob Ray Melton (1923–)

Jacob Ray, son of Jacob and Lina, worked in a Galax furniture factory and was also a truck driver. He learned dulcimer making from his father, and learned to play from his mother, Lina. Jacob Ray says that when he was hardly more than four years old he used to stand behind his mother's chair, to her right, as she played. She placed the quill in his hand, let him strum, and taught him tunes.

Beginning about 1970, Jacob Ray began to make a limited number of instruments. His dulcimers show great variety in size, shape, and sound hole patterns. Most have a double bottom and old-style wire staple frets. There is no $6^{1}/_{2}$ fret, and the VSL of the instruments falls within the old 24- to 26-inch range.

Because he does not participate in contests and fiddlers' conventions, Jacob Ray's market was limited and his output was small. When I visited him in 1992, he had made only three instruments in the past two years. I encouraged him to increase his activity, and arranged for him to accompany me to the Annual Dulcimer Playing Workshop the following year.

Virginia-style playing and Galax-style dulcimers were virtually unknown at the workshop when Jacob Ray came in 1993. His instruments and his playing created a sensation. He brought eight dulcimers with him, and sold all of them off the back of his pickup truck within fifteen minutes of his arrival. When he returned in 1995, the workshop presented him with an award for his contribution to the preservation of the traditional arts in America.

Library of Congress Recordings

Raymond Melton had the good fortune to be extensively recorded on three occasions beginning in 1965, with the recordings being deposited in the Library of Congress. These recordings constitute by far the Library's largest holdings of any dulcimer player. I have listed these sessions but have not provided the individual titles of the numerous tunes that were recorded. In the sessions, he is frequently accompanied by various other musicians.

I have provided individual listings for recordings by Jacob Ray Melton and Ruth Russell that were made along with the recordings of Raymond Melton in the 1965 session. I have also listed several recordings made in this session by Velma Nester Musser, a winner in the Galax Old Fiddler's Convention dulcimer contest in 1937, 1939, and again in 1974 (see appendix C).

In 1992, Jacob Ray Melton made a cassette entitled *Jacob Ray Melton (Galax Style Dulcimer)*, which he sells for $10 plus $3 postage and handling (1996 price). It can be ordered from Jacob Ray Melton, Route 3, Box 183, Galax, VA 24333, phone (703) 236-4543.

1340–1373   34 12-inch disks recorded by John A. Lomax, Bess Lomax, and Ruby Terrill Lomax at the Old Fiddlers' Contest, Galax, Virginia, October 1937.

1340 A1   "Dream of the Miner's Child." Sung with dulcimer by Mrs. Lina Melton.

1340 B1   "Liza Jane." Sung with dulcimer by Jacob (Jake) Melton.

1343 A4   "Blind Child's Prayer." Played on dulcimer by Myrtle Melton.

1343 B2   "Arkansas Traveler." Played on dulcimer by Raymond Melton.

1343 B3   "Brown Eyes." Played on dulcimer by Blanch Melton.

1343 B4   "Liza Jane." Played on dulcimer by Jake Melton.

1347 AZ   "Goin' Down the Road Feelin' Bad." Played on dulcimer by Ray Melton.

4784–4947   163 16-inch and 57 12-inch disks recorded by Alan Lomax, Joseph Liss, and Jerome Wiesner in Georgia, North Carolina, Tennessee, and Virginia in July and August 1941.

Includes dulcimer players Ray Melton on "Cindy," Jacob Melton on "Sally Ann," and Blanch Melton on "Old Joe Clark."

12,396–12,397   Two 10-inch tapes of instrumental folk music of Virginia and North Carolina, recorded by J. Scott Odell, Division of Musical Instruments, Smithsonian Institution, 1964–1965.

12,396   One tape containing dulcimer music. Recorded in Galax, Virginia, August 15, 19, and 20, 1965. Thirty-eight tunes played by Raymond Melton, accompanied in some instances by other musicians. Also:

12,396 A   "Goin' Down the Road Feelin' Bad." Played on dulcimer by Ruth Russell with Roscoe Russell on baritone ukelele.

12,396 A   "Dream of the Miner's Child." Same.

12,396 A   "Walking in My Sleep." Played on

dulcimer by Jacob Ray Melton with
Roscoe Russell on ukelele.

12,396 A   "Fortune." Same.

12,396 A   "Golden Slippers." Played on dulcimer by Jacob Ray Melton.

12,396 A   "Ebenezer." Same.

12,396 A   "Cripple Creek." Played on dulcimer
by Jacob Ray Melton with Roscoe
Russell on ukelele and vocals.

12,396 A   "Walking in My Sleep" Same as
above.

12,397   Recorded on August 18, 20, and 22, 1965.

12,397 A   "Sweet Sunny South." Played on dulcimer by Velma Nester Musser (Mrs.
Stark Musser) of Galax, Virginia, with
Corbett Tipton on banjo. August 20,
1965.

12,397 A   "Train on the Island." Same as above.

12,397 A   "Train on the Island." Played on dulcimer by Velma Nester Musser.

12,397 A   "If You See That Girl of Mine." Same
as above, with Corbett Tipton on
banjo.

12,397 A   "Train on the Island." Same as above.

12,397 B   "Goin' Down the Road Feel' Bad."
Played on dulcimer by Jacob Ray Mel-
ton with Roscoe Russell on ukelele.
Galax, Virginia, August 22, 1965.

12,397 B   "Ebenezer." Same as above.

12,397 B   "Down in the Levee." Same as above.

12,397 B   "Soldier's Joy." Played on dulcimer
by Jacob Ray Melton.

18,474–18,706   232 7-inch and 15-inch reels. Songs, instrumental
music, and interviews recorded in North Caro-
lina and Virginia by Blanton Owen and Tom Car-
ter, 1973–1974.

18,546, 18,547, 18,548, and 18,549 contain thirty-two songs and
tunes played by Raymond Melton with various
other musicians.

21,363–21,829   Thirty-nine cassettes and 428 tapes. Recorded in North Carolina and Virginia by various collectors for the Blue Ridge Parkway Folklife Project of the American Folklife Center, August–September 1978.

21,749, 21,750, 21,751, 21,752, and 21,771 contain 44 tunes played by Raymond Melton with various other musicians.

Figure 3.1   Jacob Ray Melton with one of his double-bottom dulcimers. The other persons are, left to right: Erin Curtis; the author's daughter, Koyuki; and Jacob Ray's wife, Dainease. Photo taken in 1993.

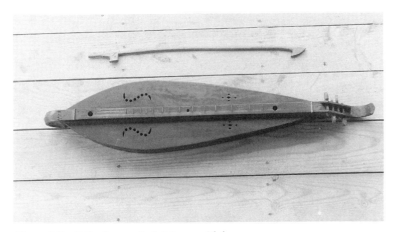

Figure 3.2   Polly Sumner's dulcimer, with bow.

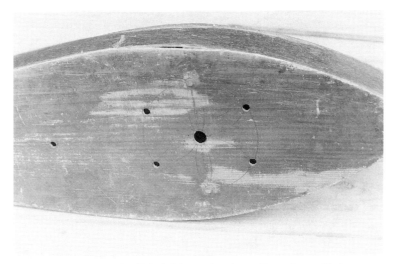

Figure 3.3   Bottom of Polly's dulcimer, showing pattern of sound holes.

Figure 3.4   Tailpiece of Polly Sumner's dulcimer.

Figure 3.5   Virgil Melton in front of Harmon's Western Wear, Hillsville, Virginia, holding dulcimer owned by Amon Melton and perhaps made by him.

Chapter 3

Figure 3.6   Bottom view of Amon Melton dulcimer, showing sound holes in bottom, semicircular tailpiece into which three large holes have been drilled, and indentations cut into the scroll to accommodate the turning of the mechanical tuners.

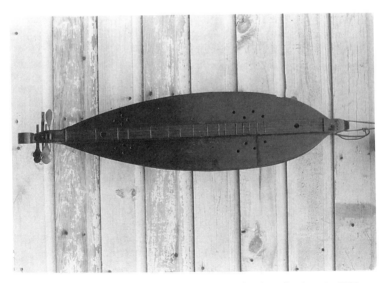

Figure 3.7   Dulcimer made by Amon's younger brother, Stephen, in 1891.

Figure 3.8   Jacob Melton, with two of his dulcimers and a wooden-head banjo.
Courtesy Jacob Ray and Dainease Melton.

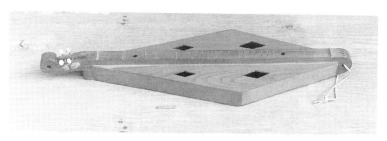

Figure 3.9   Dulcimer made by Raymond Melton, in the Harmon Museum.

Figure 3.10   Raymond Melton playing with musician friends at a drive-in near Galax, Virginia, 1977. The author is playing harmonica. Shizuko Smith.

4

The Pattern That Traveled on Horseback: Old West Virginia and North Carolina Traditions

West Virginia and the "Huntington Maker"

In the early 1990s, I set myself the task of trying to discover the identity of the mysterious person who made hourglass-shaped dulcimers in Huntington, West Virginia, in the latter part of the nineteenth century. Happily, I was successful.

Most nineteenth-century dulcimers were made by mountain craftspersons who made just one or only a few. But the "Huntington maker" apparently ran a small dulcimer-making business, complete with printed labels, mail-order merchandise, and probably a sales and distribution network of itinerant peddlers. His activities spread knowledge and use of the dulcimer throughout West Virginia and western North Carolina, with a spillover into Ohio. The design of his instruments was widely adopted throughout the area. Yet by the time of the post–World War II folk revival, knowledge of this person's activities, his instruments, and even his name was entirely lost.

First Clues

Among the instruments that Allen Smith found during dulci-
mer-hunting fieldwork in Appalachia (see chapter 2) were seven
attractive dulcimers of identical pattern and design—all apparently made by the same person. They had hourglass-shaped bodies with heart-shaped sound holes—the type that most people
associate with the word "dulcimer" today. Their bodies featured
a long, slightly inward-turning curve between the head and the
upper bout or bulge, as if the upper part of the body had been
pulled like taffy. The heads were deeply fluted, and the pegs had
squared-off rather than rounded flanges. On the back of the instruments, there were three little "feet" to facilitate playing on a
table.

These dulcimers were painted in various colorful patterns. Several had black and red swirls or painted graining. A blue or green
strip and a series of stenciled numbers ran down the fret board.
On two of the instruments, flowers were painted in the strumming area.

Most significantly, the maker of these folk creations had no intention of remaining anonymous. Inside the lower right sound
hole of several of them is a light-colored place where a label had
once been affixed. Portions of a printed label remained in three
of the instruments. On two of these, the words "Huntington, W.
Va." could be seen. And along the ragged top edge of one label
there appeared four letters, "C P RD." Were these part of the
maker's name?

The Search Begins

Two circumstances offered a time line. The state of West Virginia was created in 1863, so instruments with labels reading
"Huntington, W. Va." could not have been made earlier than that.
Curiously, in 1889 a Huntington dulcimer without a label entered
the collection of the Metropolitan Museum of Art. Reflecting the
low level of knowledge of American folk art at that time, the museum cataloged it as an eighteenth-century instrument from Germany.

Studying the spacing of the letters "C P RD," Allen Smith surmised that the C was the first letter of the maker's first name,
and he very shrewdly guessed that the last name was probably

Prichard. In Springhill Cemetery in Huntington, Allen found a gravestone for a C. N. Prichard, who was born in 1839 and died in 1904. A Prichard family genealogy, *Descendants of William Prichard*, published in 1912, lists this person as Charles Napoleon Prichard. It includes the names of members of his family but provides no other information.

Was the person buried in Springhill Cemetery the "Huntington dulcimer maker"? Allen spent days searching old records of the City of Huntington and of Cabell County in which it is located, but found nothing.

Hatfields and McCoys?

Some years later, in 1988, I found and bought a damaged, weatherbeaten Huntington dulcimer in a Washington antique shop. It contained no label, but there was an unrelated curious circumstance. An allegedly notarized piece of paper dated 1973 that accompanied the instrument said that it had once belonged to Elias "Bad 'Lias" Hatfield, of the feuding Hatfields and Mc-Coys. The document is a silly forgery, but what about the tale itself? The famous feud began in 1882. The Hatfields lived about fifty miles from Huntington, and it is known that Bad 'Lias played the fiddle. But the place where the dulcimer was made and its approximate date probably could not have been known to a forger in 1973. This instrument hangs in our living room and remains mute about where it was or what it saw and heard when it was young.

Gerry Milnes and Jimmy Costa

That's where things stood in the summer of 1991 when I talked to Gerry Milnes. Gerry is a folklorist associated with the Augusta Heritage Arts and Crafts Festival at Davis and Elkins College in West Virginia, and he provided me with a real clue.

He recalled that a mutual acquaintance named Jimmy Costa in Talcott, West Virginia, knew the whereabouts of a dulcimer with a label in it. Jimmy, a happy, ebullient person in his forties, is well known in West Virginia. He lives in a log cabin near the Greenbrier River, makes a modest income by doing carpentry, and devotes his life to gathering West Virginia historical information and artifacts.

I called Jimmy, who confirmed that he had heard of such an instrument somewhere. He would try to remember. After making one false start, he got on the right trail and discovered its whereabouts. It was in the possession of a man who had borrowed it sixteen years earlier from its owner and had never gotten around to returning it. It was arranged that the instrument would be returned via Jimmy's log cabin.

On Thanksgiving morning 1991, I entered Jimmy's cabin. It was filled with historical artifacts, and I had to be careful where I stepped. I picked up the dulcimer (figure 4.1) and eagerly looked through the lower right sound hole. There I saw a label (figure 4.2) printed in several old typefaces, all italicized except for the words "Huntington, W. Va." The paper had aged to a creamy brown, but not the tiniest chip was missing. The text, boxed inside two thin lines, read:

> From
> C. N. PRICHARD
> Manufacturer of the
> AMERICAN DULCIMER
> HUNTINGTON, W. VA.
> STRINGS 15 cts. a set
> Sent Post-Paid by Mail

Who Was He?

At last we knew the maker's name beyond doubt. But who was he? Was he the Charles N. Prichard who was buried in Huntington? Could anything be discovered about him?

By coincidence, a Huntington resident named David Mills contacted me at this time on another matter. I put him right to work. He called every Prichard in the Huntington area phone book. No luck. But he did turn up a front-page obituary in the *Huntington Advertiser* for September 12, 1904. Once again, we had been lucky; the Huntington Public Library's file of the *Advertiser*, which is now defunct, extends back only as far as 1903.

This obituary states that Charles Napoleon Prichard was born in Bolt's Fork in eastern Kentucky, served in a Kentucky cavalry unit on the Union side in the Civil War, taught school in Kentucky after his military service, came to Huntington at an unspecified date, and in 1887 launched a successful advertising paper full of humorous sayings, called *The Cricket*. He and his little publication were clearly well liked. But the full-column story included nothing about dulcimers or about anything that even related to music or craftsmanship. Was I on a wild-goose chase?

Research by Newspaper

Being a journalist and having the instincts of a journalist rather than a historian, I turned to the city's present-day newspaper, the *Huntington Herald Dispatch*. The editor of the paper's Style section was immensely interested. A reporter was assigned to the story, and the tale, complete with a picture of Jimmy Costa holding the unique labeled dulcimer, was splashed across the top of the Style section in the paper's January 12, 1992, edition. The headline read "A Musical Mystery," with the subhead "Man Searches for Lost Huntington Dulcimer Maker." The story included my phone number, with my invitation to call collect with anything that might bear the slightest resemblance to relevant information.

It seemed as if the whole city of Huntington rose up to assist me. My phone rang for days. Callers gave me information on the whereabouts of a number of previously unknown old dulcimers in the Huntington area, including another Prichard dulcimer—with no label. But for the matter at hand, three of the calls were crucial.

A rare-book and manuscript dealer named C. E. "Tank" Turley told me that his current stock contained a photo album that had belonged to Charles N. Prichard's daughter Minnie. It provided no clue relating to dulcimers, but it did contain a picture of Charles. Tank sent me the photo that appears in figure 4.3 of a kindly looking man. That Charles N. Prichard was indeed kind was soon to become evident from another caller's tale.

The next call, from a man named Norman E. Gill, was a breakthrough. Norman had been doing genealogical research on his family. One of the works he consulted was a volume entitled *1880 Census of West Virginia*, compiled by William A. Marsh. When he read the story in the *Herald Dispatch*, he checked the entries for Cabell County. Charles N. Prichard was listed, and the census taker had listed his occupation as "Manf. Music Int." This is indisputably the man who is buried at Huntington; the listing of his family in the census coincides with the listing in the Prichard genealogy.

Victory

Then, on Saturday, January 25, at 9:30 a.m., I received a call from Mrs. Golda Queen Frazier of Columbus, Ohio. Her son, who lives near Huntington, had seen the article and had sent her a copy.

"I'm eighty-six years old," she said, "and I am the granddaughter of John Wesley Prichard, Charles N. Prichard's brother. Yes, Charles made dulcimers. First he made them at Bolt's Fork, Kentucky, and then he made them in Huntington."

In her phone call and in a follow-up letter, Mrs. Frazier told me that her mother had always wanted one of her Uncle Charles's dulcimers but had never been able to obtain one. When Golda was eight years old (this would be 1913), she and her mother visited a lady named Mrs. Hicks, who owned a Prichard dulcimer. Golda's mother planned to buy it. Mrs. Hicks was poor, and Golda's mother was confident that she would sell. Mrs. Hicks played the instrument for her visitors, but she surprised and disappointed Golda's mother by refusing to sell it. Mrs. Hicks, it might be noted, was not the last poor person of Appalachia who refused to sell a beloved dulcimer to a visitor who was prepared to pay whatever the owner would ask.

Soon after calling me and writing to me, Mrs. Frazier spent an afternoon with a lady who was a childhood neighbor and has been a lifelong friend. "After she was here awhile," Mrs. Frazier wrote to me in a second letter, "I ask her if she remembered a Mrs. Hicks that lived on her Grandfathers farm. Her answer was Oh yes. On Sat. after our work was all done we kids all went to her house to hear her play the Dulcimer and sing and we would stamp our feet to the music. I said to her, they were so poor, where did she get the Dulcimer. She said a Mr. Prichard made Dulcimers and when he found she could play it. He gave her one."

A New Finding

The road of discovery soon took a remarkable turn. Bolt's Fork is located in Lawrence County, Kentucky, a short distance west and south of Huntington. I have a friend named Lea Coryell, who is a Library of Congress librarian and is also a fine old-time banjo player. During my search for information on Prichard, I kept Lea current on my findings. Lea searched for additional information in the Library of Congress.

Looking over the Library's holdings of summaries of old census records for the area, Lea came upon a summary of the 1880 Census of Lawrence County, Kentucky, that had been compiled by Opal Mae Muncy in 1979. John W. Prichard, Golda Queen Frazier's grandfather and Charles N. Prichard's brother, was listed in the census, with his wife and children. The breathtaking information was contained in the entry for John's occupation. Ms. Muncy had transcribed it as "Dulemore Maker," immediately followed by a question mark.

Checking the microfilm rolls of the original census, Lea found that the census taker's handwriting was unclear at one point, but that the entry reads either "dulcmore maker" or "dulemore maker."

I called Mrs. Frazier and asked if her grandfather John had made dulcimers. She replied no. This, of course, simply means that she had not heard of any such activity on his part. The 1880 census was taken many years before Mrs. Frazier was born.

This census entry is the oldest direct written reference to the Appalachian dulcimer that I have yet seen. Among other things, it is interesting to learn that, although Charles N. Prichard spelled the word "dulcimer" on his labels the way that we spell it today, the word was apparently pronounced "dulcimore" by his brother or by the census taker, a pronunciation that is still widely heard in the Southern mountains.

Did the brothers work together? One guesses that they did, with John and Charles both making instruments and Charles doing the selling.

And there is another question—one of the great questions of dulcimer history. In 1871, a twenty-one-year-old farmer named James Edward Thomas, who lived in Letcher County, Kentucky, some seventy-five roadless mountain miles south of Lawrence County, began to make dulcimers. We have already mentioned him in the previous chapter and will tell his story in chapter 5. Did Thomas and either or both of the young Prichards ever meet? Whether they ever met or not, did Ed see or know about John's and/or Charles's dulcimers? Or did John and/or Charles learn about dulcimers from seeing one of Ed's? No one knows. The Cumberland Mountains, which are full of secrets, will almost certainly keep this one.

North Carolina and "The Stranger From the West"

Now, let us change scenes. In June 1994, I sat on the porch of Ray and Rosa Hicks's house, on a slope of Beech Mountain near Banner Elk, North Carolina. Ray was born in this house and has lived in it all his life. The house was built by his father, Nathan Hicks (1896–1945), with lots of help from his neighbors, in 1914. It is now the oldest house on Beech Mountain. A year earlier, Nathan had married his first cousin Rena. She was then thirteen years old.

By the standards of today's lifestyles, Ray, Rosa, and their son, Ted, who lives with them, have few needs. They grow vegetables on their mountainside land. The house is heated with wood-burning stoves, and Rosa does all the family cooking on a wood-burning cook stove. Ray and Ted chop the wood, stacking it in large piles on the porch and near the house. There are some loose boards on the porch floor, but no one minds. I was simply warned where not to place the little ladderback chair that was cheerfully brought out for me when I arrived unannounced. Arriving unannounced is the only way you can arrive. They have no phone.

Ray is a member of a western North Carolina family that has been supplying field collectors with folk songs and folklore for more than sixty years. Various family members were also makers and/or players of fretless banjos and dulcimers. A fascinating book about this clan, entitled *The Last Chivaree: The Hicks Family of Beech Mountain*, by Robert Isbell, was published by the University of North Carolina Press in 1996. Much of the book is devoted to material secured during many hours spent with Ray, Rosa, and Ted.

Ray's father, Nathan, was a well-known North Carolina dulcimer maker and player. The photo reproduced here as figure 4.4, taken in 1938, shows Nathan holding one of his dulcimers, with members of his family (see also figure 4.5). What readers can easily see is that the pattern of the dulcimer strongly resembles that of the dulcimers made by Charles N. Prichard in West Virginia. The dulcimer exhibits the long reverse curve of the body running from the head to the upper bulge or bout that is a major feature of Prichard's pattern. Allen Smith calls this "sloping shoulders."

By contrast, old dulcimers from the Cumberland mountains of

Kentucky made by James Edward Thomas, have "broad shoulders"—that is, a short straight or convex line running from the head to the upper bout. This difference in body patterns is an important key to the geographical origins of old hourglass-shaped instruments.

The Stranger from the West

The West Virginia dulcimer pattern found its way into western North Carolina in the 1880s. Some old West Virginia dulcimers, other than those made by Charles N. Prichard, share their "sloping shoulders" pattern with the instruments made by Prichard. But only Prichard is known to have made dulcimers in any quantity, and only his instruments achieved significant dissemination. It is an odds-on likelihood that the original dulcimer to enter the Beech Mountain area of western North Carolina was a Prichard. According to local legend, the agent of transmission was a mysterious "Stranger From the West."

According to the most widespread version of the legend of The Stranger, a person who was not a native of the district passed through the region on horseback about 1885. In some versions of the story his name is given as Millard Oliver but no one really knows. He stopped at the little mountain home of Eli Presnell, his wife, America, whom everyone called Americy, and their four-year-old son, Nineveh, whom everyone called Ninivey (figure 4.6). The stranger requested a night's lodging, and the kind mountain couple unhesitatingly offered it. The traveler unpacked his horse, including a dulcimer that he was carrying. Eli, who had never seen or heard of dulcimers, was fascinated. As the stranger and the family sat together that evening, it seems likely that he played it. With the stranger's permission, Eli examined the instrument and made a tracing of it.

Eli certainly made one dulcimer from this tracing and may have made two or more. One of the "maybes" is reported to have been owned by a farmer named Roosevelt Presnell, who died in 1992 in his nineties. I first heard of this instrument one or two years later, but could not find it.

The one about which there can be no doubt was made by Eli for little Ninevey. There is a story that Ninevey used it as a sled. Whether or not that is true, it is definitely true that he lived all his life in the house that had been owned by his parents, that he kept the dulcimer all his life, and that he often sat on his porch playing it. An article on Ninevey and his dulcimer, which appeared in a newspaper in Johnson City, Tennessee, in 1959, is reprinted in appendix D.

When Nineveh died in 1965 at age eighty-three, the dulcimer passed to his granddaughter, Mrs. Ida Harmon of Boone. It is illustrated in figure 4.7. The pattern and measurements of this instrument do not perfectly duplicate those of Charles N. Prichard's dulcimers, but they are close enough so that the differences could reflect an individual maker's idiosyncracy. Moderate adaptation in the use of patterns was as common as, or more common than, exact replication.

As we shall see, dulcimers made by Nathan Hicks and other members of the Hicks family in the Beech Mountain area also reflect the West Virginia/Eli Presnell "sloping shoulders" pattern. Measurements of all these instruments appear in appendix A, where they can be compared.

The Hicks Family

First, some brief genealogy. The progenitor of the Hicks mountain clan was David Hicks (dates of birth and death unknown), who moved to the Watauga River wilderness in what is now Watauga County, western North Carolina, before or during the Revolution. The earliest written reference to him is in local tax records for 1778. David had two sons, Samuel, born in 1753, and David, born in 1756, and three daughters. David had fourteen children; his family moved to Indiana in 1817. Samuel, known in family lore as "Big Sammy," had five sons and four daughters. These children were the ancestors of today's western North Carolina Hicks families.

One of Big Sammy's sons was Samuel II or "Little Sammy" (born sometime between 1798 and 1800, date of death unknown). Little Sammy had four sons, two of whom were killed in the Civil War. One of the other sons, Andrew, had a son named Samuel, known as "Sammy III" (1848–1929).

Sammy III's Sons

With Sammy III's sons, we arrive at dulcimer makers. This generation became adults after the Stranger passed through and Eli had made one or more dulcimers. Two maker/players were Benjamin "Ben" Hicks (1870–1945) and Roby Hicks (1882–1957). Their brother, James Brownlow (1872–1949), is also reported to have made one or more dulcimers, but no instruments survive.

In the late 1970s, Lucy Long did extensive interviewing of Hicks family members and other local persons as part of her research for a Ph.D. thesis on the dulcimer in western North Carolina. The thesis is entitled *The Negotiation of Tradition: Collectors, Community, and the Appalachian Dulcimer in Beech Mountain, North Carolina.* Among the types of information that Lucy sought was information that might shed light on the early history of the dulcimer in the area after Eli Presnell made his instruments. Roby Hicks and his wife, Buena Vista ("Buny"), provided some old evidence.

Roby and Buny were married when Roby was fifteen and Buny was thirteen. Both said in independent interviews that when Buny was eleven, thirteen-year-old Roby came courting, carrying a dulcimer, which he showed her how to play. Roby was thirteen in 1898–1899—about fifteen years after the Stranger from the West passed through. Unfortunately, this instrument of Roby's youth has not survived, nor has any information about who might have made it.

The only dulcimer definitely made by Roby that I was able to locate was made in 1932. The instrument closely follows the Eli Presnell/West Virginia "sloping shoulders" pattern.

Some Old Dulcimers that Are Hiding

Apart from this information from Roby and Buena Vista, little is known about the history of the dulcimer in western North Carolina between the time that Eli Presnell made his first instrument and the 1930s.

Leonard Glenn, a transitional dulcimer maker described in chapter 6, said that a local man named Mac Presnell brought an old dulcimer to him many years ago to be repaired. Mac is now deceased and the whereabouts of the dulcimer are unknown. Ray Hicks said in the early 1990s that, some eighteen to twenty years previously, a member of the Farthing family, another large mountain clan, brought an hourglass-shaped dulcimer to him whose top and bottom were still joined by the end blocks but whose "hoops"—sides—were missing. The instrument had no sound holes. Ray's brother Floyd replaced the sides and cut heart-shaped sound holes in the top. The owner of the instrument is deceased and the dulcimer has disappeared.

Ben Hicks and His Children

Roby's brother Ben Hicks is a key figure, as much for who he taught and influenced as for his own work. The Hicks family genealogy says,

> Ben, as he was called, made a living by farming and gathering herbs. He was a talented woodworker and increased his income from the sale of wooden spoons, bowls, three-pronged toasting forks and dulcimers.

Edd Presnell, another transitional dulcimer maker described in chapter 6, married Nettie Hicks, who was Ben's daughter and Nathan's sister. Edd told me that Ben made a number of dulcimers; Edd's estimate at different times ranged from "a few" to "many." The instrument shown in figure 4.8 is the only one that has thus far been recovered. It was made by Ben in 1935–1936 as a wedding present for Edd and Nettie, who were married in 1936.

The reverse curve from the head to the upper bout shows it to be one more progeny of the instrument carried by the Stranger from the West. But, in typical mountain fashion, Ben has freely modified the old pattern, making it shorter, higher, and chunkier, and eliminating the overlap of the top and bottom panels over the sides.

As a child in the 1920s, Nettie learned to play from her father, Ben, and she became one of the finest traditional players. Edd learned to make dulcimers by copying the instrument made by Ben that is shown here.

Nathan Hicks

Ben's son Nathan was making dulcimers by the 1920s. It is not clear that he received his pattern from Ben. His instruments closely resemble his Uncle Roby's 1932 dulcimer. In fact, Nathan and Roby often worked together, and at this remove in time it may not always be possible to know which of them made what.

There was no market for dulcimers in Nathan and Roby's

world. However, in the late 1930s, word of Nathan's dulcimer making was carried outside Appalachia by folk song collectors Maurice Matteson and Frank and Anne Warner. Nathan began to sell a moderate number of dulcimers to people in New York. Roby joined him to create a little dulcimer enterprise. Nathan charged his customers $5 for the instruments. Roby made some and sold them to Nathan for $3, giving Nathan a $2 profit. Edd Presnell also made a few instruments for Nathan. Everybody was happy including, undoubtedly, the customers.

A similar set of circumstances occurred later when Frank Profitt, who was Nathan's son-in-law, achieved national recognition as a folksinger. Frank, who had more orders for dulcimers than he could fill, commissioned Leonard Glenn to make some for him, which he sold as Frank Profitt dulcimers. Such joint efforts appear to reflect a culture in which a fine product was often seen as more important than the exact way in which it was produced or the person who produced it.

Once, Nathan shipped two dulcimers to New York buyers. Coy Rominger, the postal rider, carried them down the mountain by horseback in his mail sacks. When the instruments arrived in New York, both were broken and were returned by the customers. The post office paid Nathan $5 each for them, which was the amount for which they were insured. Roby went to work on the instruments and fixed them up as good as new. Once again the dulcimers journeyed down the mountain in Coy's mail sacks. This time they arrived in New York intact, and the customers happily dispatched their checks!

Old-Time Player

Nathan loved both to make dulcimers and to play them. A number of pictures show Nathan sitting on his porch or in family gatherings, with his dulcimer on his lap. Leonard Glenn told me that Nathan carried a dulcimer when he rode his horse. It probably hung from the saddle horn. It was in a sack, Leonard said. At anyone's request, and perhaps even without a request, Nathan would dismount, unlimber the dulcimer, sit down, talk, and play.

Ray told me that one time in the 1930s when there was no money at all in the house, Nathan took his dulcimer down to Banner Elk, sat down at an intersection in the middle of town, played his dulcimer, and sang. ''One man stopped, and then another,'' Ray said. Soon the crowd was blocking traffic and Nathan had a nice hatful of change. But the police were not amused. ''They said they would let him go this time,'' Ray said, ''but they told him not to do it again.''

Beech Mountain Folk-Songs and Ballads

In 1936, Maurice Matteson, a folk song collector, published a small book entitled _Beech Mountain Folk-Songs and Ballads, Collected, arranged, and provided with piano accompaniments by Maurice Matteson._ This book contains the words and music to twenty-nine songs and ballads collected by Matteson in the Beech Mountain area of Western North Carolina in 1933, eight of them contributed by Nathan. The book includes a photo of Nathan holding one of his dulcimers.

Matteson was a classically trained singer and musician who taught music at the University of South Carolina. In 1932, he attended a summer music camp at Lees-McRae College in the Beech Mountain area of western North Carolina. There he met a New Jersey high school music teacher named Mellinger Henry, who was a folk music enthusiast and who had already collected the texts to many folk songs in the Beech Mountain area and elsewhere. Henry could not transcribe musical score. In 1934, Henry published a book of the texts that he had collected, entitled _Songs Sung in the Southern Appalachians, Many of Them Illustrating Ballads in the Making._ The book included the texts of eleven songs that Henry had collected from Nathan's wife Rena.

Henry told Matteson that the Beech Mountain area was a gold mine of old songs. Intrigued, Matteson did a little scouting around and discovered that Henry was right. Matteson and Henry worked together to produce _Beech Mountain Folk-Songs and Ballads_, with Matteson preparing the musical score and Henry editing the texts.

Of Nathan's eight contributions, he provided the words for only three of them, with another informant providing the tunes. For the other five he provided both text and tune, playing his dulcimer. To the best of my knowledge, these are the earliest reliable transcriptions of traditional Appalachian dulcimer tunes that we possess.

Here are Nathan Hicks's eight contributions to *Beech Mountain Folk-Songs and Ballads*:

1. "George Colon." A version of "George Collins," Child Ballad No. 85. Text and tune from Nathan Hicks, July 31, 1933.
2. "Florilla." Text from Nathan Hicks, tune from Mrs. J. E. Schell, July 15, 1933.
3. "Little Mohee." Text from Nathan Hicks, tune from Edward Tufts, July 25, 1933.
4. "The Rosewood Casket." Text from Nathan Hicks, tune from Edward Tufts, July 25, 1933.
5. "Groundhog." Text and tune from Nathan Hicks, August 2, 1933.
6. "A Wedding Song." Text and tune from Nathan Hicks, August 5, 1933.
7. "The Blue-Eyed Boy." Text and tune from Nathan Hicks, August 5, 1933.
8. "Broken Engagement." Text and tune from Nathan Hicks, August 5, 1933.

By the time that he finished *Beech Mountain Folk-Songs and Ballads*, Matteson had became strongly interested in both field collecting of folk songs and in concert performance of the material that he had collected. He used a Nathan Hicks dulcimer in his presentations.

Matteson also interested Anne and Frank Warner in Nathan Hicks and his dulcimers. In her book, *Traditional American Folk Songs from the Anne and Frank Warner Collection*, Anne says that, in 1938, shortly after she and Frank married, they were living on West 10th Street in New York.

> In the spring of that year [she writes], through Ralph Fuller, a high school and college friend of Frank's, we met a professor from South Carolina, Maurice Matteson, who had just come to New York from a song-collecting trip in the southern mountains. He had brought back with him a dulcimer made by Nathan Hicks of Beech Mountain, North Carolina. . . . We wanted very much to have a dulcimer, so we wrote to Nathan Hicks to see if he would make one for us, which he did. (p. 8)

Ordering a dulcimer from Nathan Hicks led to the Warners' first trip to the Beech Mountain area to visit the Hicks family in July

1938. This, in turn, led to a lifelong friendship between the Warner and Hicks families, which is beautifully described in Anne's book, complete with quotations of letters from Nathan, and songs learned from him, Rena, their son-in-law Frank Profitt, and others in the Beech Mountain area. The Warners sent a little financial help to the hard-pressed Hicks household when they could, plus bundles of old clothing at Christmastime. "It helped so much," Rosa told me. Rena and Nathan responded by sending, every Christmas, a bunch of beautiful mountain greens and galax leaves. Ray and Rosa still send it.

Family Sorrow

Despite the difficulties and privations of mountain life, Nathan derived happiness from his dulcimers, his music, his marriage to Rena, and his children, but he struggled with personal problems that included a sense of failure. He worked as a farmer and laborer, and he devised a scheme for selling oil from birch trees to companies that used it to make candy. After Nathan had devoted immense amounts of time and effort to the scheme, it failed when the courier who picked up the oil from Nathan to sell to the company was discovered to be diluting it. The company immediately stopped all dealings with the courier, leaving Nathan without a customer.

Nathan's family continued to grow, but clothing and shoes were scarce and sometimes there was nothing to eat. A deeply conscientious man, Nathan was depressed by his inability to protect his family from want. As time passed, he sometimes exhibited bad temper, and sometimes stayed away for a day or two at a time when there was no money and no food in the house. Rena, often ill from childbearing, child care, and privation, understood and did not complain, and the children understood too.

Nathan was deeply attached to his father, Ben. When Ben died on February 7, 1945, Nathan's heart and spirit broke. On February 20, 1945, he committed suicide.

After I had been talking with Ray and Rosa for several hours, Rosa rose quietly, went into the house, and emerged with a child-sized dulcimer (figure 4.9). Nathan, she said, had made it for Ray's young brother Jack, who was born in 1938. In 1952, Jack drowned in a swimming accident. The little dulcimer, a jewel of American folk art, survives as a token of love between father and son.

Library of Congress Recordings

The following are four songs sung at the National Folk Festival in 1938 by Maurice Matteson, accompanying himself on his Nathan Hicks dulcimer.

9829–9868   One 12-inch and thirty-nine 16-inch disks recorded at the National Folk Festival, Washington, D.C., by the U.S. Recording Company, in May 1938.

9851 B1   "Earl Brand." Sung and played on dulcimer by Maurice Matteson of Frostburg, Maryland.

9852 A1   "Bo Lamkin." ("Old Lincoln"). Same as above.

9861 B1   "Sweet Willy" ("Earl Brand"). Same as above.

9861 B2   "Four Nights Drunk" ("Our Goodman"). Same as above.

2735–3153   419 12-inch disks recorded by Herbert Halpert in the South between March 15 and June 15, 1939. This expedition was carried out under the joint sponsorship of the Library of Congress and the Folk Arts Committee of the W.P.A.

2854 A1   "George Collins." Sung with dulcimer by Nathan Hicks, Rominger, North Carolina.

2855 A1   "Ground Hog." Same as above.

2855 B1   "Bo Lamkin." Sung with dulcimer by Nathan and Rena Hicks.

2865 A3   "Pretty Polly" ("Cruel Ship Carpenter"). Sung with dulcimer by Nathan Hicks. Rena Hicks tunes the dulcimer before the song.

8772–8851   Eighty 16-inch disks of North Carolina folk songs recorded by Frank C. Brown of Duke University in the 1920s, 1930s, and 1940s.

Includes Rena Hicks singing "George Collins" and "Barbara Allen" accompanied by Nathan Hicks on dulcimer.

15,261–15,384 105 disks, various sizes, and nineteen tapes (seventeen 7-inch, two 5-inch). Folk music recorded by Anne and Frank M. Warner in Massachusetts, New Hampshire, New York, North Carolina, Vermont, Virginia, West Virginia, the Middle West, and the Bahamas, 1940–1966.

15,262 "George Collins." Sung by Rena and Nathan Hicks with Nathan on dulcimer. Beech Mountain, North Carolina, 1940.

15,262 "Blackjack David." Same as above.

15,262 "The Brown Girl." Same as above.

15,262 "Cindy in the Springtime." Played on dulcimer by Nathan Hicks with Frank Profitt on guitar.

15,262 "Roundtown Gals." Played on dulcimer by Nathan Hicks with Frank Profitt on guitar and vocal. (Dulcimer very faint.)

15,262 "Old Joe Clark." Same as above.

15,263 "Johnson Boys." Same as above.

15,263 "Fly Around Pretty Little Miss." Same as above.

15,263 "Groundhog." Same as above.

15,265 "Coming 'Round the Mountain." Played on dulcimer by Nathan Hicks with group vocal, men and women.

15,372 "Pretty Fair Miss Stood in the Garden." Played on dulcimer by Buna (Mrs. Roby) Hicks. 1951.

Figure 4.1   Jimmy Costa holding the only Prichard dulcimer known with a complete identifying label.

From
C. N. PRICHARD
Manufacturer of the
AMERICAN DULCIMER
HUNTINGTON, W. VA.
STRINGS 15 cts. a set
Sent Post-Paid by Mail

Figure 4.2   Facsimile of the label inside the Prichard dulcimer. Courtesy Swarthmore College Bulletin.

Figure 4.3   Charles N. Prichard. Courtesy C. E. Turley.

Figure 4.4   Nathan Hicks, holding dulcimer, with members of his family. Left to right: Ray; Willis, holding Betty; Mary, Louis's wife, holding Roger; Nathan; Nathan's wife, Rena; Nell; Anna; N.A.; Lewis. Photo taken by Frank and Anne Warner, June 1938. Courtesy Duke University Library. Used by permission of Garret Warner.

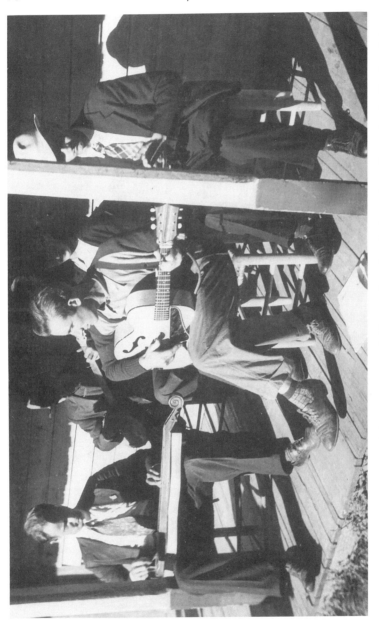

Figure 4.5 Nathan Hicks playing dulcimer, accompanied by Frank Profitt playing guitar. Photo taken by Frank and Anne Warner on the porch of Nathan's house. Courtesy Duke University Library. Used by permission of Garret Warner.

Figure 4.6   Eli Presnell (1845–1937) and his wife, America (1844–1936), who offered a night's lodging to "the Stranger from the West" when he passed through the Beech Mountain area in 1885. Courtesy Clifford and Maybelle Glenn.

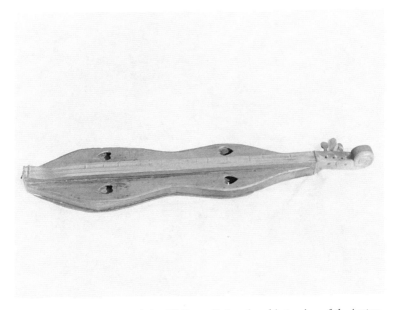

Figure 4.7   Dulcimer made by Eli Presnell, based on his tracing of the instrument carried by "the Stranger from the West." The head is a replacement made by Leonard Glenn in the 1950s.

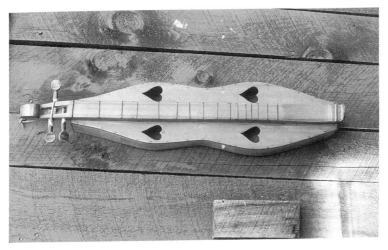

Figure 4.8   Dulcimer made by Ben Hicks, no later than 1935. The pegs are replacements made by Edd Presnell.

Figure 4.9   Rosa Hicks holding the child-sized dulcimer that Nathan made for his son Jack.

5

Dulcimers of Yesterday in the Cumberlands

Old-time dulcimers of the Cumberland Mountains are narrow-bodied, hourglass-shaped instruments of great beauty. In figure 5.1, a Prichard dulcimer from West Virginia, made in the approximate period 1880–1900, hangs on the top, and Dulcimer #18, made by Jethro Amburgey of Hindman, Kentucky in 1929, hangs on the bottom. By contrast with the West Virginia pattern, old-time dulcimers from Kentucky's Cumberland Mountains are smaller, and have "broad shoulders"—that is, the pattern moves out in a straight line or convex curve from the peg head to the upper bout. The sound holes are usually hearts. Because of the difference in the pattern, the upper sound holes are substantially closer to the peg head in Cumberland dulcimers than in West Virginia dulcimers.

The fret boards of the dulcimers made by Charles N. Prichard of Huntington, West Virginia, are hollowed out and two long slots are cut in the instrument's top underneath the fret board, to make the fret board part of the sounding box. The fret boards of old Cumberland instruments are solid sticks of wood attached to the instrument's top, which is a single panel of wood with no openings other than the sound holes.

The fret boards as well as the bodies of Cumberland mountain dulcimers are narrow. As can be seen in figure 5.1, the instruments are bridged in such a fashion that the bass and middle strings are close together. A wider space separates the middle and melody strings, providing room for the use of a wood or quill noter on the melody string. Small staple-style frets run under the melody string. The other two strings cannot be fretted. Despite the smaller overall size of the Cumberland pattern, the vibrating string length of both Cumberland and West Virginia dulcimers is the same—about 28 inches.

James Edward Thomas, the earliest Cumberland mountain maker of whom we have a record, and Charles N. Prichard of West Virginia, both began to make dulcimers shortly after the Civil War. It is not known whether either of these makers saw the other's instruments and modified the other's pattern to suit himself, or whether they worked from a common early prototype of the hourglass design, or whether they worked from different prototypes.

The example of transitional dulcimer maker Edd Presnell of Banner Elk, North Carolina, shows that one can begin by making instruments in one style and end up making them in another style, with the change not being inspired by a new prototype. Edd's first dulcimers, made in the 1930s, followed the narrow-shouldered, wide-bodied West Virginia/North Carolina pattern that was used by other Beech Mountain dulcimer makers. Over a period of about ten years, he changed his pattern to a narrow body with broad shoulders, similar to the Cumberland mountain design (see chapter 6).

The broad-shouldered Cumberland mountain design with heart-shaped sound holes had an immense influence on the post–World War II urban folk revival. Because of his relationship to Hindman Settlement School beginning in the early years of the twentieth century, Thomas enjoyed early access to eastern seaboard markets. Jethro Amburgey, Ed's protégé, made dulcimers that were virtual duplicates of the Thomas dulcimers, and lived to provide old-style Cumberland instruments to folk revival players after World War II. The Kentucky traditional singer Jean Ritchie brought an Amburgey dulcimer to New York in the late 1940s and became a well-known performer during the folk revival. The Cumberland mountain instrument became the layman's idea of a dulcimer.

Evidence points to "Uncle Ed" Thomas as the progenitor of the Cumberland pattern. We will begin this story with him. We will then discuss Josiah Combs, an interesting early player; Hindman Settlement School and Jethro Amburgey, who was the school's shop teacher; and, finally, a rather unlikely subject that could be called "the politics of dulcimers."

James Edward "Uncle Ed" Thomas

It is hard to tell whether Uncle Ed (figure 5.2) is buried in Knott or Letcher County. On a mild, blue-sky-and-white-cloud day late in December 1992, my daughter, Koyuki, and I stood in a weed-tangled little graveyard high on the Cumberland ridge that runs along the border between Knott and Letcher. The dirt-and-boulder road that struggles up the mountain from the Letcher County side is nearly impassable. Few people ever come.

In the graveyard, two small footstones mark the graves of James Edward Thomas and his wife, Sarabelle. There are no headstones. A weathered board leans aslant over the head of one of the graves. Nothing is written on it. But from the graveyard, beautiful vistas extend over the Cumberlands, symbolic, perhaps, of this old-time mountain man's durable legacy.

Home, Family, Occupation

According to information that appears in the book *Knott County, Kentucky History & Families, 1884–1994*, the Thomas family shares two characteristics with many other old-time mountain families: the family arrived in Appalachia at an early time, and it includes an admixture of Indian blood.

The earliest family member of whom there is a record is James Edward Thomas, the grandfather of the dulcimer maker, who shares the dulcimer maker's name. Grandfather James lived in Ashe County, which is in the northwestern tip of North Carolina. In either 1805 or 1815 he married Lucy Proctor, who was part Cherokee Indian. Their children included Greenberry Thomas, born about 1820, and James Thomas, born about 1826, who does not appear to have carried his father's middle name. Grandfather James died in Ashe County in 1831.

After Grandfather James's death, Lucy moved from Ashe County, North Carolina, to Letcher County, Kentucky—from a wild and primitive world to one that was even more wild and primitive. Her reasons are not known. Greenberry and James went with her. "She says that they were called the white Indians," the *Knott County History* states.

In 1849, James married Mary Madden of Letcher County. Records exist of eleven children. One was James Edward Thomas, the dulcimer maker. He was born in 1850 and died in 1933.

In 1884, Knott County was formed from parts of Perry, Letcher, Floyd, and Breathitt counties. The county seat was established at Hindman, a town that, in 1886, had seventeen houses and a population of about one hundred. Hindman's population today is about nine hundred. It remains the county seat. Neither Hindman nor the county as a whole has a traffic light, apart from yellow flashers at two intersections.

Uncle Ed and his family lived in a log cabin in Knott County, on Big Doubles Creek, in a little community called Bath, which once had a post office. Labels inside Thomas dulcimers usually state that they were "manufactured" in Bath, Kentucky.

You will not find Bath on the *Rand McNally Road Atlas* map of Kentucky, so let me help you. On the Rand McNally map, you can see Kentucky Route 160 proceeding south from Hindman about four miles to Littcarr. From Littcarr, and not shown on the Rand McNally map, little Kentucky route 1410 heads east, takes the Cumberland ridge head-on, and winds precariously over it to Colson, on Route 7 in Letcher County, which the map shows.

Before climbing the mountain to Letcher, 1410 runs beside a sparkling stream called Little Carr Fork on the right. Big Doubles Creek branches off Little Carr to the right, and a dirt road follows it. The few houses along the dirt road constitute what now exists of Bath. Somewhere in the "holler" up Big Doubles—no one could tell us exactly where—stood the log cabin from which dulcimers were shipped to such places as New York and London.

The 1870 U.S. Census of Letcher County lists Thomas, age twenty, as a farmer, and gives the age of his wife, Sarabelle, as fifteen. The 1910 census of Knott County gives Thomas's occupation as house carpenter, which several of our informants confirmed. The 1910 census also states that Uncle Ed could read and write but that Sarabelle could not.

Uncle Ed was a highly skilled woodworker, and he made many things in addition to houses and dulcimers. Hassie Hicks Martin of Hindman, Kentucky, who knew Uncle Ed when she was a child, said that he also made furniture such as chests of drawers and pie safes.

The Dulcimer Maker

Allen H. Eaton's book *Handicrafts of the Southern Highlands*, published in 1937, states that Thomas began to make dulcimers in 1871. Thomas's practice of numbering and dating his instruments indicates that this date is right or close to right.

The oldest Thomas dulcimer yet recovered is number 469, dated January 10, 1891. It is illustrated and described in Allen Smith's *Catalogue of Pre-Revival Appalachian Dulcimers*, page 82. In the early 1980s I bought this instrument from its owner/restorer, Mr. J. E. Matheny. The most recent Thomas that has yet been found was acquired in 1995 by Don and Betty Brinker of Latrobe, Pennsylvania. It is number 1465, dated February 1931, and was therefore made when Uncle Ed was eighty or eighty-one years old. It shows no diminution in his woodworking skills. The Brinkers obtained it from its original owner, to whom it was given by his aunt and uncle when he lived with them for several months in 1932 or 1933 at their home in Blackey, Letcher County, Kentucky, when he was a boy.

Uncle Ed was a neighbor and good friend of Balis Ritchie, father of Jean Ritchie. Jean says that in 1923, McKinley Craft, another friend and neighbor, sent a Thomas dulcimer to McKinley's kinsman Joe Craft in Arkansas, and that Lynn Elder, the pioneer Arkansas dulcimer maker, based his pattern on this instrument. She also provides a down-to-earth explanation of why Uncle Ed painted many of his instruments black. "Did you know," she wrote to me, "that Uncle Ed told us that the reason he painted some of his dulcimers black is that he had might-near a whole bucket of paint left over from painting his barn?"

Beloved Neighbor

The portrait of Uncle Ed that emerged from the accounts of the older people with whom we spoke was of an exceptionally well-liked, warmhearted man with a notable sense of humor. Lona Ward Gibson spoke for many others. "They say he was a wonderful person," she told us. "Everything I ever heard about him is good."

Mal Gibson, age ninety-two, a neighbor and friend of Uncle Ed's who is not directly related to Lona, adds that Uncle Ed had a sly sense of humor—something that is clearly reflected in the carved head of Josiah Combs's dulcimer, which we will soon describe. In her book *Dulcimer People*, Jean Ritchie quotes James Still, the well-known Kentucky novelist and poet who has lived on Dead Mare Branch, near Bath, since 1929: "He [Thomas] was a unique personality. Anticky. Comical. Liked a joke on himself as well as others. Delighted in pulling a rusty (practical joke)."

Popular Salesman

In her book *Dulcimer People*, Jean Ritchie says that Uncle Ed traveled through Knott and Letcher counties in the summertime, carrying his dulcimers on a little cart, playing for anyone who would listen, staying overnight with families who were happy to exchange lodging for some dulcimer music, and seeking sales. He sold his instruments for a few dollars each or traded them for some food. All of this was confirmed by a number of older people with whom we spoke, and we learned of several persons who had bought instruments from him during his peregrinations.

We also learned that Uncle Ed sold his dulcimers at the general store in Hindman. The store's proprietor, Elijah Hicks, was one of Uncle Ed's innumerable friends, and did not charge him for leaving his instruments to be sold. Elijah was the father of Corinne Hicks and Hassie Hicks Martin.

Fine Player

Uncle Ed himself was undoubtedly an excellent player with a good repertoire, and he loved to play. Mal Gibson says that Uncle Ed used to sit on the porch of the Thomas log cabin and play to his heart's content.

I interviewed Lone Madden, Uncle Ed's seventy-eight-year-old grandson, by phone. Lone heard his grandfather play many times. He named five tunes that, according to his recollection, Uncle Ed played: "Cripple Creek," "Sourwood Mountain," "Groundhog," "Pretty Polly," and "Darling Corey." The presence of "Pretty Polly" on this list suggests that Uncle Ed may have understood the Dorian and/or Aeolian tuning for the dulcimer. On the other hand, maybe not. I have heard Edd Presnell's wife, Nettie (see chapter 6), play the Dorian tune "Shady Grove" on the Dorian scale but with the instrument tuned Ionian.

A Folk Woodcarver

In addition to being a woodworker and cabinetmaker, Uncle Ed was a carver. Two informants told us that he carved owls and other birds. One said that an owl carved by Uncle Ed had stood on a cornerpost of their porch railing for many years, but then had disappeared. No one that we talked to knew where any of his carvings could now be found.

Josiah H. Combs

We stopped at Berea College on our way to the mountains, and there we learned in the early 1990s, a Thomas dulcimer had been donated to the college by the widow of D. K. Wilgus, the UCLA folklorist. The instrument had belonged to the pioneer Kentucky folklorist Josiah H. Combs (1886–1960). This dulcimer, dated October 28, 1903, is the second-oldest Thomas that is currently known, and is also, by some nine years, the oldest Thomas yet discovered that has heart-shaped sound holes. It is not numbered in any place that is visible to external inspection. It should be noted that Thomas dulcimer number 469, described above, the oldest known, is also not numbered in any place that is visible. H. E. Matheny, who restored the instrument from damaged and disassembled pieces, found the number written on the bottom surface of the fret board. This instrument, made in 1891, has diamond-shaped sound holes at the upper bout and crescent-moon-shaped sound holes at the lower bout.

Figure 5.3 shows Combs with his Thomas dulcimer. Figure 5.4 shows the instrument's head, which is carved as the head of a dog with its tongue sticking out.

Josiah H. Combs, born and raised in Cumberlands near Hindman, was the star student in the little common school that he attended, and read voraciously on his own. He was one of two members of the first graduating class of Hindman Settlement School, receiving his diploma in 1904.

The *Knott County History* contains an informal autobiographical essay written by Combs. It is undated but, from internal evidence, was written about 1914 when he was twenty-eight. Regarding his childhood, Combs says:

> During vacation from school, when I was at work on the farm, I usually carried a book of some sort up to the cornfield with me. When we sat down to rest, I would read. I "finished" many of the classics in this way. People would say, "W'y, that 'ere boy's a reading hisself plum' to death; he'll never get over hit."

Books were scarce in his world and there were no libraries. For a year or two he walked a mile to Hindman, whose population was about 300, every night to sell the *Cincinnati Post* to earn money to buy books.

Katherine Pettit and May Stone, the founders of Hindman Settlement School, spent some time in the area before launching the school and quickly became acquainted with the bookish mountain boy. One day Pettit encountered him walking along the road barefoot, reading a book. "Well, what are you reading now?" she asked. "Hist'ry!" Combs cheerfully replied.

When Hindman Settlement School was officially launched in 1902, Combs was one of the initial enrollees. The date of his dulcimer suggests that he may have acquired it while still a student at Hindman. At the school, Pettit took down a number of his songs and ballads and forwarded them to the *Journal of American Folklore*, where they were published in 1907.

After graduating from Hindman, Combs received the first scholarship awarded by Kentucky University—now called Transylvania University—to a Hindman graduate. The *Lexington Herald* offered to cover his other expenses. Carrying his dulcimer, Combs journeyed to Lexington with a corn cob pipe and less than $5 in his pocket, and was enrolled.

At the University, Combs shared his knowledge of Kentucky mountain folklore with Dr. Hubert G. Shearin, the young head of the English department. Together they compiled *A Syllabus of Kentucky Folksongs*, which was published in 1911. Combs followed this with two other books, *The Kentucky Highlanders* (1912) and *All That's Kentucky: An Anthology* (1915).

After graduation, Combs taught in several high schools and colleges, served overseas in World War I, and then enrolled at the University of Paris, where he graduated summa cum laude with an M.A., earned a Ph.D. from the Sorbonne, and married a French woman. His doctoral thesis, written in French, was a study of the ballads and folksongs of his native Kentucky. It was published in Paris in 1925 under the title *Folk-Songs du Midi des Etats-Unis.*

After returning from France, Combs was professor of French and German at the University of Oklahoma, head of the Department of Foreign Languages at Texas Christian University, and head of the French Department at Mary Washington College of the University of Virginia. He retired in 1956 and died four years later.

Throughout his career Combs collected Kentucky songs, ballads, and folklore, and played his 1903 Thomas dulcimer. As far as I can determine, he was the first native of the mountains to carry the dulcimer and its music to audiences beyond Appalachia. "Wherever I went, the people always gazed at the strange musical instrument I carried under my arm," he writes.

In his essay, Combs describes his journey to Cleveland to give a paper at a meeting of the American Dialect Society. "I picked my dulcimore at the evening 'smoker,' " he says. At a meeting of The Kentuckians of New York City, held at Delmonico's in 1913, he explained the dulcimer in an after-dinner speech. "Can you pick that thing?" one of the Kentuckians asked. "I wouldn't pack 'er ef I couldn' pick 'er!" Combs grinned. And he proceeded to prove it.

In 1940, at Texas Christian University where he was teaching, Alan and Elizabeth Lomax recorded Combs playing his Thomas dulcimer, for the Library of Congress. The recordings are listed at the end of this chapter.

Hindman Settlement School

By the time that Hindman Settlement School (figures 5.5 and 5.6) was founded in 1902, people had been filtering into the remote valleys and ridges of the Cumberlands for more than one hundred years.

Some came by way of the Wilderness Road. After the road crossed the sparkling waters of the Cumberland River Ford at present-day Pineville, Kentucky, it continued west into Kentucky's bluegrass country. However, one could leave the road here, turn northeast, follow the hollows and dry creek beds between the Cumberland mountain ranges, and enter a virgin mountain world. Game and timber were plentiful, and a family could help itself to a little land that no one claimed, along a creek bottom or on a hillside. This is what some hardy people did.

In Letcher County and its surrounding area, people also arrived through Pound Gap, a pass in Cumberland Mountain about fifty miles north of Cumberland Gap, near present-day Jenkins, Kentucky. At Pound Gap, Virginia shares its border with Letcher County.

The people who settled the Cumberlands lived in relative isolation throughout the nineteenth century and preserved an immense treasure of folklore, speech, music, and folkways that have kept folklorists busy ever since. Mountaineers made by hand much of what they needed and wanted, including musical instruments, and eked out a self-reliant existence in "The Land of Do-Without." They also developed a fabled sense of humor, laughing at the great difficulties of mountain life in stories and song.

However, things did not become easier with the passage of time. As the nineteenth century progressed, game was depleted and timber was increasingly exhausted. Big mountain families, who typically occupied one- and two-room windowless log cabins, quickly exceeded the capability of the little hardscrabble farms to provide. As farms were divided among sons, the difficulty increased. Travel and communications were immensely difficult. And even if there had been roads to markets, the mountain people had almost nothing to sell. There was little access to health facilities or to education. Disease, infant mortality, and illiteracy rose to high levels.

These conditions were brought forcefully to the attention of the outside world in the latter years of the nineteenth century by a series of violent family feuds in the mountains, which claimed many lives. Problems in the Cumberlands became a major interest of women's clubs, church groups, and civic groups in Kentucky's bluegrass region during the 1890s. Both in the mountains and beyond, there was widespread belief that training and education were the keys to providing the mountain people with a better life.

In 1899, with backing from the Kentucky Federation of Women's Clubs and the Women's Christian Temperance Union, May Stone, Katherine Pettit, and two other women, all from financially comfortable families in Eastern Kentucky, made the two-day, forty-mile trip by "jolt wagon" from the railhead to the mountains, and conducted summer educational activities for adults and children in tents set up on hillsides overlooking the village of Hazard in Perry County. The activity created a sensation in the area. Local people begged the women to return, and discussion of a school was immediately begun. Pettit and Stone conducted similar summer camps in nearby locations in 1900 and 1901, with equal success. Then, with funding from Eastern Kentucky patrons, with small sums from the mountain people, and with eagerly donated labor, they launched Hindman Settlement School.

The school opened in the fall of 1902 with 162 pupils, on a donated piece of land on the edge of the little town that included the small meadow at the forks of Troublesome Creek and the adjoining narrow hillside. From its inception, it provided quality education up through high school, a level of education that was at that time unobtainable in the area. Students living beyond walking distance, which was most of them, boarded at the school. Students paid what they could; ability to pay was never a factor in the acceptance of students.

In addition to providing formal primary and secondary school education, Stone and Pettit launched community activities, including encouragement of local skills such as basket making, weaving, and spinning. Efforts were made to find markets beyond the mountains for homemade crafts. A "Fireside Industries Department" was organized for this purpose.

Hindman's administrators and teachers were largely drawn from the educated middle and upper class of New York and New England. Most were young women graduates of such colleges as Smith, Vassar, Holyoke, and Wellesley. Typical was Elizabeth Watts, who arrived in 1909 to serve as a primary-level teacher. Her stepfather was head of the English department at Phillips Academy, Andover, Massachusetts, and was chief book reviewer for the *Atlantic Monthly*. She remained to become assistant director of the school in 1924, and director after May Stone passed away in 1946. Katherine Pettit left Hindman in 1912 to found Pine Mountain Settlement School in an even more remote area of the Cumberlands.

Hindman struggled with a perpetual waiting list. Some adults and children didn't wait; they walked. In 1912, Elizabeth Watts wrote to her mother:

Yesterday three new little girls arrived. They came from Floyd County above Beaver Creek and they walked fifty long miles with their father who will have to walk it back again, poor man! They left home one morning getting here the next day at noon . . . the least girl was only six. They had hardly anything to eat along the way for wherever they stopped the folks had no bread.[1]

One of the school's major interests was traditional Appalachian music. It served as a center for gathering and re-disseminating folk songs, and hosted folk-song collectors who gathered many old songs and tunes from the students.

The teachers and administrators quickly became acquainted with Uncle Ed and his dulcimers. To them, the dulcimer's physical beauty, its mist-enshrouded origins, which they assumed traced back to Elizabethan England, the perpetuation of both the instrument and its playing methods in the mountains without outside influence, and the body of traditional music that was played on the instrument, made it the perfect expression of traditional mountain culture. Teachers bought dulcimers from Uncle Ed and secured many sales for him among their families and friends in New England and along the Eastern seaboard. The dulcimer became a prominent symbol of both mountain culture and the Settlement School.

The School assigned dulcimer making and playing to an important place among the mountain arts to be preserved, fostered, and integrated into its educational program. Students made dulcimers in the school's shop and played them, as a central feature of the School's emphasis on encouraging mountain children to value their traditions rather than to regard them as inferior to modern education and new ways.

Jethro Amburgey (1895–1971)

Jethro Amburgey was the next-to-last child of Wiley Amburgey, who had twenty-one children by two wives. Wiley was born in Virginia or North Carolina; Jethro wasn't sure. At the age of four, Wiley arrived in Letcher County in 1827, with his father Ambrose and family. Ambrose settled on Little Carr Creek near Wolfpen Stream, built a log home, raised first one large family and then another, and learned to be a surveyor.

Jethro began school in an old log schoolhouse near his home.

After a few years, he heard of Hindman Settlement School, which was ten miles away. His parents agreed that he could enroll with the understanding that he would "work his way." Hindman enrolled the bright, serious lad in the sixth grade.

When America entered World War I, a number of Hindman boys became restless. They often talked together about the battles in France, which they regarded as heroic adventure. One day early in 1918, several of them, including Jethro, left the school, walked twenty-two miles to Hazard, and enlisted. After three months of training, Jethro was sent overseas with the 38th Infantry, 3rd Division, as a member of a machine gun company. He saw action at the Second Battle of the Marne in July 1918 and was wounded in the Argonne.

After the war, Jethro returned to Hindman, graduated in 1920, and remained at the school as shop teacher and basketball coach, staying until the early 1930s. He then went back to school at Morehead State University, receiving a bachelor's degree in 1935. From 1940 to 1944 he served as Knott County Superintendent of Schools, but found politics stressful and did not stand for reelection. He continued to teach at various high schools, finally retiring after a teaching career of some thirty-three years. In 1989, eighteen years after his death, he was elected to the Knott County Hall of Fame.

Knott County remembers Amburgey as one of its fine educators and public officials, but the world remembers him for something that Knott County residents often teased him about—making dulcimers. When he returned to Hindman after World War I, he worked in the shop several hours a day to make a little money while completing his schooling. Uncle Ed Thomas often dropped by the shop, passing the time of day and picking up some glue or sandpaper for his dulcimer making. One day Jethro told Uncle Ed that he would like to learn to make dulcimers, and asked Uncle Ed if he would provide him a set of patterns. Uncle Ed realized that sooner or later this could mean competition. He said yes, if Jethro would pay him more for a set of patterns than Uncle Ed ordinarily received for a finished instrument. Jethro happily agreed. The next day Uncle Ed showed up with a set of patterns made from pasteboard, and the deal was made.

Amburgey said in a 1971 interview that he began to make dulcimers "long about the last year of high school." The likely time

is therefore the fall of 1919 or the spring of 1920. He followed
Uncle Ed's practice of dating and numbering most of his instruments. (See figure 5.7.)

The earliest Amburgey so far found that has a number and
date on a paper label inside the lower left sound hole is number
18, dated May 16, 1929. This is the instrument hanging below the
Prichard dulcimer in figure 5.1. It belonged to Margaret Motter,
a graduate of Hood College and a teacher at Pine Mountain Settlement School from 1928 to 1932. Figure 5.8 shows two Amburgeys, number 90 made in 1938 and number 467 made in 1961.

Number 467 is typical of many instruments made by Amburgey as his sales began to increase during the post–World War II
folk revival. "He got a little careless," one museum curator said
to me. There is a pronounced symmetry problem in number 461,
and the pre–World War II purfling, which requires time and care
to execute, is missing. The fret board is also somewhat wider than
that of #90 (figure 5.9).

Over a period of time, Amburgey encountered significant
problems with having the top and/or bottom panels of his dulcimers split. In the early forties, to solve the problem, he shifted to
a thin, three-ply plywood for making the top panels and bottoms
of his instruments.

In a 1963 interview that appeared in the *Louisville Courier-Journal*, Amburgey said, "I'm selling more dulcimers now than I ever
thought of selling several years ago. . . . I ship them practically
everywhere." The price at that time was $35. Orders continued to
flood his mailbox. In February 1971, he made number 1191, which
is now in the possession of a relative, Renee Combs. According
to one report, he completed number 1369 on November 25, 1971,
the day he died, but if this instrument exists, its whereabouts are
unknown, and Jethro's son Morris doubts that the report is correct.

In addition to making dulcimers, Jethro was a fine player. Morris says that Jethro used a long piece of paper, folded over several
times, for striking the strings. Photos taken at Hindman Settlement School also show him picking the strings with his fingers.
Morris says that his dad's favorite songs were "Barbara Allen"
and "Bury Me Beneath the Willow."

All buyers of Amburgey dulcimers, from the beginning to the
end, received a genuine old-time Cumberland dulcimer in the

original Thomas pattern. Amburgey always used the old short frets and string spacing that Thomas was using a hundred years earlier, and no 6^1/$_2$ fret ever put in an appearance on his fret board. Today, all Amburgey dulcimers belong to a vanished past.

Dulcimers and "The Politics of Culture"

It is a bit difficult to believe that there could be such a subject as "the politics of dulcimers," but in fact there is. It is a subset of a lively field of academic debate that goes under the name of "the politics of culture."

In essence, proponents of the "politics of culture" critique of society state that people belonging to the nation's power elite, who were ostensibly involved in helping less-powerful social groups such as Appalachian mountaineers and Native Americans, actually imposed their own notions and values on these cultures. Hard-liners say that the "helpers" gave crumbs to the disadvantaged, virtually as part of a conspiracy with other advantaged groups to fleece the parties ostensibly being helped. Proponents of these views often believe in the broad explanatory power of a model of society whose predominating feature is a one-way street on which oppressors work their will on the oppressed.

Applying the critique to Hindman Settlement School and its interest in the dulcimer, scholars such as David Whisnant, author of *All That Is Native and Fine: The Politics of Culture in an American Region*, offer the view that the administrators and teachers at Hindman did one or both of two things: They imposed prevailing upper-class cultural values on the mountain children and their parents, and/or they kept the mountaineers tranquilized with quaint things like dulcimers while the coal barons robbed them.

With regard to dulcimers, Whisnant states that the administrators of the school chose the dulcimer over the banjo for a priority place in Hindman's activities because they preferred its gentility to the rowdy songs and social settings with which the banjo was associated. For Whisnant, this constitutes what politics of culture advocates call cultural imposition.

In examining these interesting views, we can begin by acknowledging two facts. First, romantic attitudes toward the Ap-

palachian mountain people were widely prevalent among the
nation's more literate and educated classes during the first half
of the twentieth century, and the dulcimer became associated
with these romantic ideas. Second, these notions were often related to a belief in the racial superiority of native Anglo-Saxon
stock over that of people from other nations and cultures.

Mountaineers were seen as sharing in that intrinsic superiority.
Although currently in reduced circumstances, they were nevertheless "cousins of Lincoln." Folklorists such as Jean Thomas and
novelists such as John Fox Jr., in his book *The Little Shepherd of
Kingdom Come*, published in 1903 and one of the first American
books to sell over a million copies, couldn't find flowery enough
language to describe these highland sons and daughters of Mer-
rie England. Neither, for that matter, could Theodore Roosevelt
in *The Winning of the West*.

It followed that mountaineers had dropped behind the proces-
sion simply as a result of unfortunate historical accidents. All
they needed to take their rightful place among America's May-
flower families and power elite was a decent education and a bit
of opportunity. Educated and empowered, they might even serve
as a welcome bulwark against the tide of "foreign" immigration.

Much of this dithering is silly and plenty of it is reprehensible.
With these things granted, there remain ample grounds to believe
that the class struggle model of the politics of culture will produce results that are hardly an improvement in terms of accom-
modating the full truth.

Whisnant's model is of an all-powerful segment of society
working its cultural will on groups that are powerless to resist.
One of the most interesting features of this model is its ostensible
sympathy for the allegedly powerless people, combined with a
condescendingly low opinion of their capability for relating to
external cultural forces in their environment.

Folklorist Lucy Long, author of the Ph.D. thesis, *The Negotiation
of Tradition: Collectors, Community, and the Appalachian Dulcimer in
Beech Mountain, North Carolina*, cited in the preceding chapter, is
among many students of culture who believe that the cultural
imposition model is flawed. The model, she states, "tends to por-
tray Appalachian culture as adulterated by outside intervention.
The interactions between outsiders and mountain natives, however, have always been a two-way dialogue."[2] In contact between

cultures, an interaction occurs in which both sides act and both possess leverage. Negotiation, not imposition, Long states, is therefore the concept that produces the most comprehensive and accurate description of what occurs in the interaction.

The Dulcimer and Banjo at Hindman

The statements that Hindman was biased against the banjo and that its special interest in the dulcimer illustrates the insidious workings of cultural imposition, are worthy of a detailed look.

First, the dulcimer, which developed in isolation as a mountain handcraft, was a more appropriate symbol of Hindman and its purposes than the banjo. The banjo did not originate or develop in the mountains. It was brought to America by black slaves, who developed it in plantation settings. From there, the instrument migrated to the national minstrel stage in the early 1840s. The mountains were its last stop; it entered Appalachia after the Civil War. Banjos were made in factories and were sold through the Sears Roebuck and Montgomery Ward catalogs. Banjo playing was a national activity that was doing fine on its own in the mountains and everywhere else without any need for Hindman's help.

In the early twentieth century the dulcimer was in a different situation. Dulcimer making and dulcimer playing were endangered regional arts. Hindman could and did play a valuable role in preserving the instrument and its music.

Second, it is difficult to document Whisnant's statement that Hindman's administrators were biased against the banjo, on which much of his analysis depends. I have trouble reconciling this alleged bias with statements such as the following, from Katherine Pettit's diary:

> Some of the people thought it was wrong to have any kind of music but meetin' house songs. We mistakenly asked a young man to bring his banjo and give us some mountain music. A good sister hastened to urge us not to have "banjo pickin'" and said some of the people were saying that we could not be good if we liked it.[3]

This quote not only raises questions about bias against the banjo, but illustrates Lucy Long's concept that cultural contact produces interaction, and that a correct account of it must describe the in-

teraction. Virtually any quotation taken from Pettit's diary provides additional evidence.

And, finally, the banjo was in fact present at Hindman. One of
the school's early experiences with traditional folk music came
when a girl student played "Barbara Allen," accompanying herself on a banjo. An old photograph taken at Hindman shows four
students with dulcimers and a fifth with a gourd banjo. If its presence was begrudged, Whisnant does not prove it and the school
denies it.

With regard to the making of dulcimers by some students in
the school's shop, this fit well with a vocationally oriented man-
ual arts program in carpentry and woodworking. Making dulcimers involves measuring, cutting, finishing, and joining long
boards and pieces of wood. It has more educational value in a
high school woodworking program than making banjos, which is
to a greater extent a carving exercise and involves other problems
as well.

Let us envision that the school had given a prominent place to
banjo making in its industrial arts activities. Making banjos requires killing small animals to make the banjo heads. Until very
recently, the heads of mountain banjos were made from the skins
of groundhogs, squirrels, and cats. Banjo making would have re-
quired the killing by the use of firearms, of substantial numbers
of squirrels and groundhogs, which were larger and therefore
more desirable but less common. Presumably, cats would be off-
limits. Many more animals, especially squirrels, would have to be
killed than were used because bullet holes in any place other than
the heads would render the small skins unusable, and even
mountain boys rarely hit small, fleet-footed animals in the head.

Shooting the animals is followed by skinning. The skins are
soaked in a solution of wood ashes for several days, giving the
lye from the ashes time to act on the fur. The skins are then removed from the vat and the fur is scraped off. It smells terrible
but it works. The scraped skins are nailed up on the side of a
building to dry in the sun. They can then be cut and stretched
over the head of the instrument.

Cultural impositionists perhaps forget that, first and foremost,
Hindman was a school. The correct criterion for what to include
in the program of a school is the educational value of the activity.
Both as a symbol and for its education value in shop work, the
dulcimer was a sensible choice.

Library of Congress Recordings

The Library of Congress Archive of Folk Culture has no record-ings of Uncle Ed Thomas, and as far as I know, he was never recorded by anyone else. The Archive does have a single record-ing of Jethro Amburgey; a single recording of McKinley Craft, a dulcimer maker who knew Uncle Ed and learned to make dulci-mers from him; several recordings of Balis Ritchie, Jean Ritchie's father, who learned to play from Uncle Ed; eight recordings by Josiah H. Combs; three recordings (two songs) by Jean Ritchie; and seven recordings by Edna Ritchie Baker, Jean's sister. These recordings are listed below. Jean Ritchie has made numerous commercial recordings, of which many are currently available, and Edna has also made several commercial recordings.

1374–1601	228 12-inch disks recorded by Alan and Eliza-beth Lomax in Kentucky, September and Octo-ber 1937.
	1551 B1 "The Girl I Left Behind Me." Played on dulcimer by McKinley Craft of Cody, Kentucky. Recorded in Cody, Ken-tucky.
3942–4087	146 12-inch disks recorded by John A. Lomax and others in Alabama, Georgia, Louisiana, Mis-sissippi, and Texas.
	3950 A1 "I'm Climbing up Jacob's Ladder." Sung with dulcimer by Professor Jos-iah Combs. Recorded by John A. and Bess Brown Lomax in Fort Worth, Texas, September 1940.
	3950 A2 "Corn Likker." Same as above.
	3950 A3 "Cluck Old Hen." Same as above.
	3950 A4 "Slago Town." Same as above.
	3950 B1 "William and Dina." Same as above.
	3950 B3 "Barbara Allen." Same as above.
	3950 B4 "Jack Wilson." Same as above.
	3951 A1 "Lord Thomas" Same as above.
10,882–10,895	Fourteen 7-inch tapes of fiddle, banjo, and dulci-mer music and songs recorded by Wyatt Insko in

eastern Kentucky and southeastern Ohio in July 1954.

10,887   Fragment, unidentified. Played on dulcimer by Balis Ritchie. Viper, Kentucky, July 20, 1954.

10,887   Same fragment. Same as above.

10,887   Religious piece. Same as above.

10,887   "Lonesome Creek." Same as above.

10,887   "Skip to My Lou." Same as above.

10,888   "Red River Valley." Played on dulcimer by Jethro Amburgey, Hindman, Kentucky, July 1954.

11,307–11,309   Three 10-inch tapes. Anglo-American songs and ballads from New England and California; English and Gaelic songs and ballads from Cape Breton Island, Canada, Spanish-American songs from southern California. Recorded by Sidney Robertson Cowell.

11,307   "I Wonder Where Moria's Gone." Sung and played on dulcimer by Jean Ritchie.

11,307   "I Wonder Where Moria's Gone." Same as above.

11,307   "The May Carol." Same as above.

15,571–15,576   Six ten-inch tapes. Copy of twenty-three 7-inch tapes of Kentucky Folk music and lore, recorded by Frank Traficanti and students at the University of Kentucky, 1972. Includes Buell Kazee, Pleaz Mobley, Lily Mae Pennington, Edna Ritchie, and a church service. LWO 7284.

15,573   "Goodbye Liza Jane." Played on dulcimer by Mrs. Edna Ritchie Baker. Winchester, Kentucky, March 11, 1972.

15,573   "Liza Jane" and "Groundhog" played on "sweetheart dulcimer" (dulcimer with double fret board) by Mr. Floyd and Mrs. Edna Ritchie Baker.

15,573   "Little Reckless Boy." Played as duet. Same as above.

15,573   "Hymn No. 99." Same as above.

15,573   "Turkey in the Straw." Same as above,
with dancing doll.
15,573   "Sourwood Mountain." Same as above.

Notes

1. Quoted in Rhonda George England, *Voices From the History of Teaching: Katherine Pettit, May Stone and Elizabeth Watts at Hindman Settlement School, 1899–1956.* Unpublished Ph.D. dissertation (Lexington: University of Kentucky, 1990), 140.
2. Long, 35.
3. England, 71.

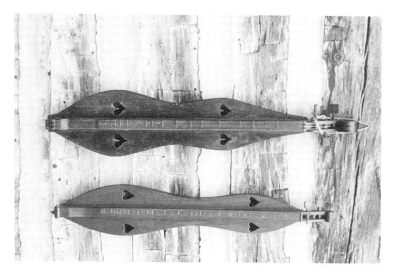

Figure 5.1   The West Virginia and Kentucky patterns compared. Top, dulcimer made by Charles N. Prichard, Huntington, West Virginia, 1880–1900. Bottom, dulcimer #18 made by Jethro Amburgey, Hindman, Kentucky, dated May 16, 1929.

Figure 5.2 Uncle Ed on the grounds of Hindman Settlement School, with his walking stick and a dulcimer. Probably 1920s. Courtesy Hindman Settlement School.

Figure 5.3   Josiah H. Combs with his 1903 Thomas dulcimer. Probably 1910–1915. Courtesy Mike Mullins.

Figure 5.4   Head of the 1903 Thomas dulcimer, showing dog's head with tongue sticking out. Kara Beth Brunner.

Figure 5.5 Hindman Settlement School student with dulcimer. Note home-made fiddle in background. Courtesy Hindman Settlement School.

Figure 5.6   Pauline Ritchie, Jean Ritchie's sister, playing in the doorway of a log cabin on the school grounds. Of the fourteen Ritchie children, Una, Pauline, Jewel, May, Ollie, Mallie, and Raymond attended Hindman Settlement School. Courtesy Hindman Settlement School.

Figure 5.7   Jethro Amburgey playing one of his dulcimers. Note apparent finger-picking style with right hand. Courtesy Hindman Settlement School.

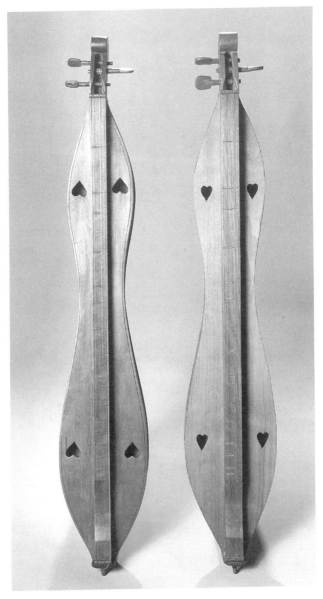

Figure 5.8 Jethro Amburgey dulcimer number 90, made May 9, 1938 (left), and number 467, made May 31, 1961. James Still Collection, Morehead State University. Eric Shindlebower, MSU Photographic Services.

Figure 5.9 Head of Amburgey dulcimer number 90. Eric Shindlebower, MSU Photographic Services.

6

Dulcimer Makers of the Folk Revival Transition

As the post–World War II folk revival began to gather momentum in the 1950s, awareness of the dulcimer spread rapidly in urban centers throughout the country. In Appalachia, several makers whose early dulcimers were purely traditional, modified their instruments to relate successfully to the needs and wants of the growing ranks of new urban players and succeeded in developing markets. Changes included substituting modern instrument fretting for the old-style staple frets; securing fully accurate fret patterns; inserting a $6^1/2$ fret in the fret boards; utilizing an increasing variety of woods; and using woods of contrasting colors for the back, sides, top, and fret boards of their instruments. These refinements were made to basic patterns that derived directly from old and early traditions, and that remained fully recognizable when they had done their work.

Of the four transitional dulcimer makers described here, two, Edd Presnell and Leonard Glenn, passed away in the 1990s. A fifth member of the group, Virginia's Jacob Ray Melton, is discussed in the context of his family's dulcimer traditions in chapter 3. These makers represent the final chapter of the story of the traditional dulcimer in the Appalachians. It is a wonderful last chapter.

Homer Ledford

Homer Ledford of Winchester, Kentucky, modified the old Cumberland dulcimer pattern in a number of ways over a period of years, and carried it into the folk revival.

Homer was born in 1927 in Ivyton, Tennessee, in the north-central part of the state, about thirty miles south of the Kentucky line. His father was a farmer; he was one of four children. His home world was mountainous, with swinging bridges across crystal-clear streams. "We had a pretty hard time, you might say, as children," Homer said as we sat and talked in the parlor of his modest home, the day after Christmas in 1992. "We didn't have a lot."

When Homer was twelve, his brother joined the Civilian Conservation Corps to bring in a little money for the family. "We finally got enough money to buy a battery radio," Homer says. "We listened to the Grand Old Opry every Saturday night until the battery went dead."

Sometime around 1938, when Homer was about eleven years old, he made his first musical instrument, a fiddle, out of a dynamite box, which he covered with matchsticks. It turned out that the glue that he ordered from a mail-order company wasn't very good and the matchsticks fell off. In 1946, he tried again. He had read in the Sears Roebuck catalog that fiddles were made of curly maple. He cut a piece from an old maple tree that grew in his father's hog lot, dried it in his mother's cookstove, and this time made a fiddle that stayed together and worked fine.

In 1946, after high school, he was encouraged to attend the John C. Campbell Folk School in Brasstown, North Carolina, while he recuperated from rheumatic fever. Then as now, the Campbell Folk School interested itself in mountain traditions, skills, and crafts. The school offered short courses in vegetable dyeing, pottery, folk dancing, folk singing, storytelling, and similar subjects that could be used in recreational programs at schools and colleges. Homer remained at Campbell off and on for two and a half years. There he learned about dulcimers and made his first instruments.

Edna Ritchie, Jean Ritchie's sister, taught at the school. Jean came for a visit, just before she went to New York. Her arrival in New York stirred up immediate interest in dulcimers. Bob Hart, manager of the handicraft shop in New York that was affiliated with the Southern Highland Handicraft Guild, sent a letter to Campbell Folk School ordering two dulcimers for the shop. Homer was known to have made a fiddle, so the job passed to him. Using an Amburgey dulcimer as his pattern, he made the dulcimers.

"They paid me $20 apiece!" Homer chortled as we talked about it more than forty years later. "I was making no money at all. I was rich!"

That was only the beginning. People who were at the school taking short courses saw the dulcimers while they were being made and before they were shipped. They ordered a total of eight more. Figure 6.1 shows Homer holding his dulcimer number 3, which was one of the eight. It is made of black walnut and butternut, which mountain people called white walnut because they didn't know its correct name. The dulcimer has the narrow body and small staple frets of the old Cumberland design. The owner recently shipped it back to Homer, saying that he should rightfully have it, and refusing Homer's delighted offer to pay a good price.

In 1949, Homer entered Berea College. Berea students, most of whom are drawn from the mountains, must work to pay for part of the costs of their education. Homer made instruments, which the school sold. At Berea he learned to make mandolins and guitars.

He also continued to made dulcimers, and began to redesign the old Cumberland pattern. He broadened and deepened the body, widened the fret board, and shortened the vibrating string length from 28 inches to $26^1/_2$ inches. These changes can be seen in figure 6.2. He laid out the fret pattern of each instrument by ear. "I made a little fret out of a wire that came all the way across and bent down the side, that I could slide under the strings—a movable fret, same size as the wire I was going to use for a fret. And I moved it along and I strummed the string until it would sound perfect, and then I'd mark it." As we will see, Edd Presnell of Banner Elk, North Carolina, did the same thing, and many other old time makers undoubtedly used this method.

Homer tuned his instruments GGC. "This is the way that Edna told me to tune," he says. And, in fact, GGC was the traditional Cumberland Ionian tuning, although the strings sound brighter if brought up to DAA, which is the usual basic tuning today. Perhaps GGC was used because it caused the instrument's major tuning to correspond with the major scale in the key of C on the piano. Homer also learned about Dorian and Mixolydian tunings from Jean and Edna Ritchie when he was at Berea.

He continued to use staple-style frets for fifteen years or more after Berea. However, Homer is a guitar player, and he wanted to fret both the melody and the middle string with his fingers instead of playing with a noter. This is the reason that he widened the fret board. He extended the frets under both the melody and middle strings. He also extended the third fret under all three strings, "so I could get a G-seventh chord." The frets continued to be of the wire staple type until the 1970s, when he finally adopted modern instrument frets running under all the strings.

He modified the shape of the peg box "to make it flow more," and also tapered the head. He changed the sound holes from hearts to diamonds. He wanted to be different, he says, and, also, he adds, diamond-shaped sound holes are easy to cut. "I made a chisel, a very, very thin chisel, that you could push four times and cut that sound hole." By the late 1960s, he yielded to the wishes of many of his customers and switched back to hearts.

An interesting feature of his redesign relates to the use of four strings. Old Cumberland dulcimers, without exception as far as I know, have three. These days, a paired melody string is common, to make the melody more audible over the two drones. Homer thinks that he is responsible for this innovation of the folk revival, but it came about in an indirect way.

About 1960, he paired his middle string. The reason related to his method of play, in which he fingered both melody and middle strings. At dulcimer gatherings, one can sometimes see today one or two Ledford dulcimers of this era, with staple frets running under two of the strings except the long one at the third fret, a doubled middle string, and diamond-shaped sound holes. They constitute living history of the transition from old to new.

It was Edna Ritchie's husband, Floyd, who urged Homer to take the next step. Homer made a dulcimer for Floyd's birthday. Floyd, however, played only with a noter. A doubled middle string, which added one more string to an already strong drone, was a net liability. Floyd dropped by to see Homer.

"How would it be, Brother Ledford," Floyd asked, "if we put that string on the outside where I could push it with my noter?"

"Well, no problem, Floyd," Homer replied.

"I didn't know what I was doing," Homer reminisced, "but I put it out there, all right. Now, Floyd and Edna were going around all over the country giving concerts. They went to the National Folk Festival, went to fairs, went to all these places, and people saw that doubled melody string, and it caught on. Then people came to me and asked how come *my* double string's in the middle. I said, that's where I started it!"

After Berea, Homer taught school in Louisville in 1955, then left and taught for nine more years in Winchester, Kentucky, where he still lives. Finally, the balance tipped to the point at which he could earn more money by making instruments than by teaching. He then turned to instrument making full time, and has been an instrument maker ever since. He can make nearly anything. His output over the years includes about twenty-five guitars, about 500 fiddles, and, as of July 1996, 5,706 dulcimers. As Homer nears his seventieth birthday, he can scarcely keep up with his orders.

Leonard and Clifford Glenn

The long reverse curve exhibited by the dulcimers made by Charles N. Prichard of Huntington, West Virginia, has been passed down into North Carolina dulcimers through two tracings, one done by Eli Presnell in 1885 and one by Leonard Glenn in the 1950s. The latter tracing brought the pattern into the folk revival.

Despite the beauty and quality of their dulcimers, Nathan and Roby Hicks's dulcimer making did not produce a direct legacy. Nathan died shortly before the post–World War II revival began. The persons in the Beech Mountain area who bridged the gap from the old to the new were Leonard Glenn of Sugar Grove, North Carolina, and his son Clifford.

Leonard, the son of Nathaniel ("Nat") and Kimmey Glenn, was born in Watauga County on December 5, 1910, and lived there until his death on April 3, 1997. The Glenns lived about a mile up Rush Branch Road, a gravel road in the vicinity of Beech Mountain. Leonard's grandfather on his mother's side was Eli Presnell, who received the Stranger in 1885 and traced his dulcimer.

Nat Glenn made fretless banjos and one dulcimer. The latter, which would be of immense historical interest, apparently no longer exists. "It was destroyed in some fashion," Leonard said.

On December 22, 1934, Leonard married Clara Ward (figure 6.3), who, Leonard said, "was raised just down the dirt road from me!" Their son and only child, Clifford, was born on December 29, 1935.

Leonard bought a tract of mountainside land from Clara's father, Robey Monroe Ward, for $20 an acre, paying it off over a period of time. He kept a horse and two cows and tilled the fields, raising beans, corn, potatoes, and tobacco. He was also an excellent carpenter and possessed many other skills, which he put to good use. As a WPA worker during the Depression, he helped to build the foundation of Cove Creek Elementary School. He worked at a sawmill on the Watauga River, and at a water-powered sawmill and grain mill at Laurel Creek Falls.

In 1936–1937, Leonard and Monroe built the small house in which he and Clara lived for the rest of his lifetime and where Clara still lives, on the land that Leonard had purchased from Monroe. The house existed for many years before any car reached it. On June 17, 1964, Clifford married Maybelle Presnell (figure 6.4). Shortly after Clifford and Maybelle were married, Leonard, his brother Howard, and Clifford built Clifford and Maybelle's small house, about twenty yards from Leonard and Clara's home.

Banjos and Dulcimers

In the early 1950s, Leonard and Clifford began to make banjos and dulcimers. They made more dulcimers than banjos, principally because of the difficulty associated with procuring a sufficient number of skins of small animals for banjo heads, which is described in chapter 5. Banjos made with the skins of small wild animals are much more appropriate as individual items made for use by the maker than they are as production items for resale. In later years, Leonard and Clifford discovered that they could buy calfskins at music stores, and these were substituted for squirrel hides. Now they use imported skins of Mexican goats, which are cheaper.

Leonard and Clifford's first dulcimers were boat-shaped; that is, they were Virginia-style, rather than the hourglass shape that was already traditional to western North Carolina. "I think I must have made it up," Leonard said, "although I might have seen one. I didn't have a pattern to go by." Leonard's first dulcimer was purchased by neighbor Ray Farthing; Clifford's, by folklorist John Putnam. John paid $20 for Clifford's dulcimer. Clifford was about nineteen when he made it. "I said to myself, 'It's the first, and it'll be the last!'" Clifford says. Fortunately, he changed his mind.

In the 1950s, the legacy of the Stranger from the West once more asserted itself. The head of Nineveh Presnell's dulcimer broke. Nineveh, who was Leonard's maternal uncle, brought the instrument to Leonard and asked if he could replace the head. Leonard put a new head on the instrument—and traced its pattern. History had repeated itself. Leonard and Clifford began to make dulcimers in the Stranger's pattern.

Subsequently, in response to customer requests for Kentucky-style instruments, Leonard and Clifford adopted Homer Ledford's basic pattern and added it to their offerings.

A third pattern that was used by Leonard for a period of time in the 1960s is illustrated by the middle instrument in figure 6.5. Lewis Hicks, one of Nathan Hicks's sons, brought a Nathan Hicks dulcimer to Leonard and asked him to make a couple of instruments from the pattern to give to members of his family. The pattern of this particular Nathan Hicks dulcimer featured a larger upper bout than Eli Presnell's dulcimer, and a slight reverse curve running from the lower bout to the foot.

At about this time, as previously noted, Leonard agreed to make some dulcimers for the old-time folksinger and instrument maker Frank Profitt. Frank requested that Leonard make instruments for him in the Nathan Hicks pattern, perhaps to distinguish them from the Glenns' standard pattern.

Leonard made a limited number of instruments in this pattern. They bear no indication that he is the maker. The instrument in the center in figure 6.5 once had the words F. P. DULCIMER lightly penciled inside the lower left sound hole. The inscription was partially obliterated during restoration, so the initial P. and the letters MER are all that remain. Leonard examined this instrument and confirmed that he made it.

Changes Caused by the Folk Revival

Leonard's and Clifford's early instruments reflected their traditional roots. For his first dulcimer, Clifford made frets out of pins with their heads cut off. After that, both Leonard and Clifford made frets out of the wire that is used for electric fences, bending pieces in the shape of staples and inserting them into the fret board. In their early instruments, the frets were short, running under the melody string only. Later, the staple-style frets were made longer, to extend under all three strings. Finally, they shifted to modern instrument frets. For the first few instruments that they made in this fashion, they took the frets out of old guitars.

Expanding Sales

Initially, there was little demand among local persons for Leonard's and Clifford's instruments. However, in the 1950s, several local retail establishments accepted dulcimers from them, and the results pleased everybody. Sales received double impetus from the folk revival and from the ever-increasing influx of tourists to what was becoming a favored vacation area. Stores in the Boone/Blowing Rock area that sold Glenn dulcimers included Ray Farthing's furniture store, Bob Harmon's Godwin Weaving Shop, the Log House, and Walker's jewelry store. On the Blue Ridge Parkway, the Northwest Trading Post at Glendale Springs took in some instruments. They moved right out into tourists' cars, and the Trading Post reordered.

Throughout this period, Leonard and Clifford continued to farm, making dulcimers and banjos in the wintertime. By the 1970s, their sales volume and reputation had reached the point at which they no longer needed to sell in the shops. From that time forward, they conducted their business from their homes, selling directly to customers who range from local buyers to enthusiasts in Japan.

Playing Methods and Songs

Leonard played both dulcimer and banjo, and so does Clifford. Maybelle plays the dulcimer. Clifford and Maybelle sometimes play duets, with him playing the banjo.

Leonard said that Nineveh played his dulcimer with a noter—"probably a match stem," he said. Leonard played "a little" with a noter, but then abandoned it. When I asked him about it, he held up his thumb, grinned, and said, "There's my noter!" Clifford also used a noter for awhile, then switched to his fingers. Maybelle uses a matchstick.

For strumming, Leonard used a piece of TV lead-in wire with the wire removed from the center. "I like my pick to be pretty limber," he said.

Clifford says that songs that he has known "as long as I can remember" include "Cripple Creek," "Old Joe Clark," "Sourwood Mountain," "Lonesome Road Blues," "Wildwood Flower," and "Groundhog."

Matching the Old and the New

As is described in chapter 4, I acquired a Prichard dulcimer in 1988. The dulcimer is shown on the top in figure 5.1. In June 1991, I traveled up the mountain road to the Glenns with a busload of persons who were attending the Annual Dulcimer Playing Workshop at Appalachian State University. I was carrying my Prichard dulcimer.

In Clifford's small living room, with workshop attendees crammed into every available bit of space, I removed the Prichard dulcimer from its bag. Clifford held up a dulcimer he had just made, and we pressed the two instruments together, back to back. It was a close match. There was an audible gasp from the thrilled audience. It was almost as if the Stranger had entered the room after more than a hundred years to say, "Yes, you've got it right!"

That night I thought about the Stranger for many hours. I conjured up the scene of his arrival, of his conversation with Eli and America, and of the unpacking of his horse.

Eli:	What's that?
Stranger:	That's a delcymore.
Eli:	Can you play it?
Stranger:	Wouldn't pack 'er if I couldn't pick 'er!
America:	I'd love to hear it. Bring it in!

On April 3, 1997, Leonard, who played the key role in bringing the Stranger's legacy into the folk revival, passed away.

Edd Presnell

Edd Presnell, son of Nathan and Lindy Presnell, was born on January 24, 1916. The family lived about a mile from the place where Edd established his own home and workshop. Nathan was a farmer and miller who operated a water grist mill on the Watauga River.

On March 17, 1935, when he was nineteen, Edd married seventeen-year-old Nettie Hicks, daughter of John Benjamin (Ben) and Julie Hicks and sister of Nathan. Edd and Nettie visited a magistrate in the evening to get their license. The magistrate obligingly rousted out a preacher at 11 at night to marry them. The preacher charged 50 cents. It added up to less than a penny a year for the years of their devoted and remarkable marriage.

Nettie's family gave the couple 129 acres of mountain land, and Edd became a farmer, a profession that he followed until about 1965, when wood carving and dulcimer making began to bring in enough money to pay the bills.

Edd and Nettie had four children—Saskie Lucille (born 1937), Baxter (born 1938), Julie Ellen (born 1941), and Marthana (born 1950). Baxter inherited the family woodworking skills. He attended Berea College for three years, then returned and built a house near Edd and Nettie's home. He did not make dulcimers, but produced a wide range of decorative woodcarvings and wood jewelry. By the 1960s, he was a full-fledged partner with his parents in a business that included the sale of dulcimers and woodcarvings.

Edd's Early Instruments

Edd's first dulcimer, which he made in 1936 shortly after his marriage to Nettie, was patterned after the Ben Hicks instrument that is illustrated in chapter 4. The dulcimer that Edd made has been lost, and other early Presnell dulcimers from the 1930s and 1940s have similarly disappeared. Edd made only a small number, because the local demand was not large and as yet he had no other market. "People used to say, 'We got no use for that thing!' " Edd told me.

Edd made his early instruments without power tools. He used an ax, handsaw, hammer, brace and bit, jack plane, and smoothing plane. He whittled the pegs, and cut the heart-shaped sound holes with a piece of sawblade that had belonged to Ben.

For these early instruments, Edd cut tops and bottoms from logs, using a handsaw or crosscut saw. They were often made from poplar logs from local log cabins. The sides were made of "wahoo," a flexible magnolia wood that he cut and bent when it was green. He poured hot water over the pieces to facilitate bending, and put them in a form until they were dry. The back was attached to the sides first, then the top, and then the head and fret board were mounted.

The instruments were fretted with wire staple frets, whose placement was determined by ear. Like Homer Ledford, Edd made some temporary frets, which he slid up and down the fret board while plucking a string to determine the placement. There was no standard nut-to-bridge string span.

Developing His Own Pattern

Edd soon made major modifications in Ben's pattern. By the 1940s, he had evolved the beautiful narrow instrument that became his trademark. He settled on a 29-inch vibrating string length, an inch longer than the old hourglass dulcimer patterns of both West Virginia/North Carolina and the Cumberlands. His pattern, Jean Ritchie said in *The Dulcimer Book*, looks "curiously like those of Ed Thomas." In 1992, when Edd Presnell was a featured guest at the Legendary Dulcimer Maker's Forum at the Annual Dulcimer Players' Workshop at Appalachian State University, and I was the moderator, I asked him the big question:

RLS: Did you know Jethro Amburgey?
Edd: Yes, I knew him.
RLS: Was the shape and pattern of your instruments influenced in any way by Jethro and his instruments?
Edd: Not to my knowledge. I developed my pattern myself.

I have no doubt of the accuracy of his answer.

The Folk Revival

In the latter half of the 1950s, things began to happen for Edd. The folk and craft revivals were taking hold, and Edd's dulcimers became part of it. In 1956, the folklorist Richard Chase launched a once-a-week folk festival at the "Horn in the West" summer outdoor drama in Boone. Edd came with his dulcimers and sold some. Also, he joined the Southern Highland Handicraft Guild in Asheville, which, in the 1950s, operated outlets in New York, the District of Columbia, Atlanta, and Knoxville as well as Asheville. The Guild sent Presnell dulcimers to its outlets, and the instruments sold. Other shops in New York, California, and Madison, Wisconsin, began to place orders. Invitations began to arrive to exhibit and sell his instruments at local and regional craft shows and craft fairs, which became increasingly popular in the 1950s. Nettie, who had learned to play the dulcimer from her father, Ben, when she was a child in the 1920s, brushed up her playing skills, accompanied Edd to the shows and fairs, and showed people how to play.

Edd bought some power tools and set up a workshop. Sometime in the latter part of the 1950s he also began to number his instruments, beginning with number 1, so that the numbers do not reflect those instruments that he made before the numbering began. The total of instruments that he made during the pre-numbering days was not large. Edd's last numbered instrument was Number 1890, which he completed early in 1994.

During the period from 1960 to 1965, Edd discontinued shipping dulcimers to craft shops, and sold only at craft fairs and from his home. At the time that he discontinued shipping instruments to the shops, orders from the shops for twenty-five dulcimers were sitting on his table. Business leveled off, but Edd had all he needed and could handle. He never advertised, but information about his dulcimers reached around the world. Presnell dulcimers went to such places as Germany, Japan, and Zaire (Democratic Republic of the Congo).

Visiting the Presnells

In the 1970s, I visited Edd and Nettie several times (figure 6.6). Getting there was an adventure all by itself. I passed through the little village of Valle Crucis, and then took North Carolina Route 194, which winds steeply up the mountainside and includes several astonishing hairpin curves. (When I drove this road with my twelve-year-old daughter Koyuki and her school friend Erin in 1990, neither of them wanted to look.) Arriving at a plateau at the top, I turned right, and soon arrived at a sign reading, "Pavement Ends." From there it was a beautiful drive over several miles of dirt and gravel roads, crossing a stream on a log bridge in the mottled sunlight, passing fabulous vistas of mountain scenery, and arriving at a turnoff marked by a small carved wooden sign reading, "The Presnells."

This road included several big ruts and boulders that slowed me to a creep. On my right, on the side of the downward-sloping hill, stood a weathered old house. I didn't learn until later that it was the house that Nathan Hicks built in 1914, which is described in chapter 4, and in which Ray and Rosa Hicks and their son Ted live. The road took me for another mile along the crest of a ridge, and ended at a simple brick ranch house of early postwar design. The house looked out on endless mountain vistas. On the left was the wooden building that housed Edd's shop. A dog of totally mixed lineage came out to greet me, wagging his tail, and Edd stood inside the house's screen door, smoking his pipe and smiling a greeting.

Three Presnell Dulcimers

When I visited in 1976, Edd had recently cut down an apple tree near his house, and had made an applewood dulcimer for a customer in Pittsburgh. Apple trees are small and can provide only a few boards long enough for the sides and back of a dulcimer. There was enough wood left from this tree to make a couple of more instruments. I ordered one, and Edd made dulcimer number 1266, dated August 29, 1976, which is illustrated in the center of figure 6.7. This dulcimer illustrates Edd's standard pattern.

While Edd's dulcimer-making trade grew, so did his fame as an Appalachian woodcarver. Pictures of him with his woodcarvings appeared in *National Geographic* and many other magazines. Increasingly from the 1970s on, at the customer's request, Edd carved decorative patterns and motifs on the tops and fret boards of his instruments, carved the pegs in the shape of dogwood flowers and birds, and even inlaid flowers made of white dogwood. Beginning in the 1980s, Nettie began to execute some of the carving on the top panels. These instruments are jointly signed by Edd and Nettie.

The two other instruments in figure 6.7 illustrate these features. The numbers show that they were made one right after the other. Edd and Nettie jointly signed them both.

The instrument on the left was made for my daughter, Koyuki, and me. The top panels are cherry, and the rest of the instrument is walnut. Dogwood flowers are incised into the top panels and fret board, and the sound holes are hearts-within-hearts. The two left-hand pegs are dogwood flowers, and the right-hand peg is a bird.

The instrument on the right (figure 6.8) was made for Shirley Leedy of Falls Church, Virginia. Shirley is a local historian and a ballad singer. The instrument is made of cherry, with dogwood flowers made of white maple inlaid into the top panels.

By the early 1960s, Edd was offering a $6^1/_2$ fret to customers who requested it. "Don't you want it?" he asked when I refused the $6^1/_2$ fret for my applewood dulcimer. "When you've got it, you can play all those pretty Christmas carols!" Beginning in the 1980s, he also deepened his strum hollow, which had been very shallow, to accommodate the use of a hard pick for picking the individual strings.

Nettie's Playing

In addition to her woodcarving skills, Nettie is a great old-time player. She can be heard playing "Amazing Grace," "Sally Goodin," and "Shady Grove" on the album *Instrumental Music of the Southern Appalachians*, Tradition TLP 1007, recorded in the summer of 1956 and reissued from time to time in cassette form.

In the early 1990s, Nettie suffered a stroke and has been confined to a wheelchair. She speaks with difficulty, and can play only by using a finger instead of a noter on the melody string, and picking just the melody string with her right hand. Her memory for tunes, however, is unimpaired.

On June 15, 1994, I visited Edd and Nettie. I put my dulcimer number 1796 across the arms of Nettie's wheelchair, and she played while Edd listened. I snapped the picture that appears in figure 6.9. When I saw the photo, I felt that it reflected the greatness of two people who virtually lived the history of the dulcimer as it emerged from Appalachian obscurity to worldwide popularity.

On August 3, 1994, Edd passed away.

Library of Congress Recordings

The Library of Congress has no recordings of Homer Ledford, or of Leonard and/or Clifford Glenn. Homer has made a number of recordings as a player of various instruments in local bands. For information, contact him at the address/phone number given in appendix D.

Leonard and Clifford play banjo and dulcimer on several cuts on the recording *It Still Lives*, issued by Foxfire in 1980 and still in print. Copies can be obtained from Clifford. Contact him at the address/phone number given in appendix D.

Nettie Presnell, one of the greatest traditional dulcimer players, was rarely recorded. Her sole appearance on a commercial recording, consisting of three tunes, is cited above. The Library of Congress Archive has two more, made by Frank and Anne Warner, for a precious total of five. Note that Buny Hicks sings with Nettie on "Johnson Boys."

15,261–15,384   105 disks (various sizes) and 19 tapes (seventeen 7-inch, two 5-inch). Folk music recorded by Anne and Frank M. Warner in Massachusetts, New Hampshire, New York, North Carolina, Vermont, Virginia, West Virginia, the Middle West, and the Bahamas, 1940–1966.

      15,367   Unidentified. Played on dulcimer by Mrs. Edd (Nettie Hicks) Presnell. North Carolina Mountains, 1951.

      15,367   "Johnson Boys." Played on dulcimer by Mrs. Edd Presnell with Roby Hicks on vocal and fiddle, and Buny (Mrs. Roby) Hicks on vocal. 1951.

Figure 6.1   Homer Ledford holding his dulcimer number 3, made in 1948. Photo taken in 1992.

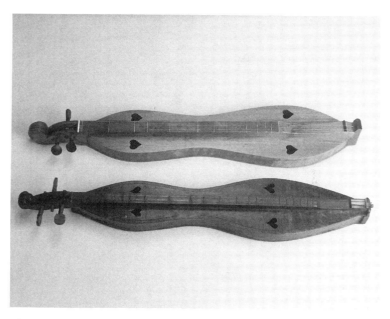

Figure 6.2   The evolution of Homer Ledford's pattern. Bottom, dulcimer made by J. Edward Thomas, Bath, Kentucky, 1903. Top, Homer Ledford dulcimer number 5498, 1992. Kara Beth Brunner.

Figure 6.3   Leonard and Clara Glenn, 1992. Leonard, an incorrigible cutup, is "left-shouldering" one of his Kentucky-pattern instruments.

Figure 6.4   Clifford and Maybelle Glenn, 1992, with one of his North Carolina-pattern instruments. This dulcimer is made of curly poplar, called "monkey-face poplar" in the mountains, with walnut head and fret board, and inlay made of holly.

Figure 6.5   Glenn dulcimers. Left, North Carolina pattern, made by Clifford in 1979. Center, Hicks pattern, made by Leonard to be sold by Frank Profitt, c. 1963. Right, Kentucky pattern, made by Leonard, 1979.

Figure 6.6   Edd Presnell, 1978, holding a six-string dulcimer that he made for his wife, Nettie, who is on the right. My wife, Shizuko, is on the left, holding our daughter, Koyuki.

Figure 6.7   Dulcimers made by Edd Presnell. Left to right: number 1795, dated August 16, 1991, made of cherry and walnut; number 1266, dated August 29, 1976, made of apple wood; number 1796, dated September 4, 1991, made of cherry and inlaid with dogwood flowers made of white maple.

Figure 6.8   Detail of dogwood inlay in Presnell dulcimer number 1796.

Chapter 6

Figure 6.9   Edd and Nettie with dulcimer number 1796, June 15, 1994.

Appendix A

Measurements of Representative Instruments

Measurements of a number of instruments described and illustrated in this book are provided in this appendix. The instruments chosen for inclusion here are important in their own right or are good specimens of representative types. These measurements will enable the reader to compare instruments, traditions, and patterns. The instruments can also be compared with the larger selection of instruments and measurements that can be found in my book, *The Story of the Dulcimer*, and in Allen Smith's book, *A Catalogue of Pre-Revival Appalachian Dulcimers*.

In the measurements given below, the abbreviation VSL stands for vibrating string length, that is, the length of the strings from the top bridge, called the nut, to the lower bridge. The reader knows from the text that the usual VSL of scheitholts is 24 to 26 inches, the usual VSL of Virginia-style dulcimers is the same, and the usual VSL of hourglass-shaped dulcimers is about 28 inches.

Chapter 2

Ache Scheitholt:

Overall length:	$37^3/_8$ inches
VSL:	$24^1/_8$ inches

Josie Wiseman's Scheitholt-on-a-Sound Box:

Length, excluding knob at
    end: $30^3/_8$ inches
VSL: $24^3/_8$ inches

Chapter 3

Polly Sumner Dulcimer:

Length:	36 inches
VSL:	$25^1/_4$ inches
Width:	$7^7/_{16}$ inches
Height of body:	$2^5/_8$ inches

Amon Melton Dulcimer:

Length:	37 inches
VSL:	$25^1/_2$ inches
Width:	6 inches
Height of body:	$2^7/_8$ inches

Steven Melton Dulcimer:

Length:	34 inches
VSL:	$25^7/_8$ inches
Width:	$8^3/_4$ inches
Height of body:	$2^1/_8$ inches

Raymond Melton Dulcimer in Harmon museum:

Length:	$36^3/_8$ inches
VSL:	$27^1/_8$ inches
Width:	$10^1/_4$ inches
Height of Body:	$2^1/_4$ inches

Raymond lengthened the VSL of his instruments to approximate that of hourglass-shaped dulcimers.

Chapter 4

Charles N. Prichard Dulcimer with Label:

Length:	$35^1/_4$ inches
VSL:	$28^1/_4$ inches

Width, upper bout:	$6^1/_{16}$ inches
Width, waist:	$4^3/_4$ inches
Width, lower bout:	$7^1/_2$ inches
Height of body:	2 inches

Eli Presnell Dulcimer:

Length:	Uncertain; head was replaced.
VSL:	29 inches
Width, upper bout:	$5^1/_2$ inches
Width, waist:	$4^1/_4$ inches
Width, lower bout:	$6^1/_2$ inches
Height of body:	$1^1/_2$ inches

For variations in the measurements of instruments that were "copied" from other instruments, see the comments under the Amburgey dulcimer below. In my opinion, the variations in the measurements of the Prichard and Eli Presnell dulcimers that are provided here fall easily within the range of variations that makers were likely to introduce in making "copies."

Ben Hicks Dulcimer:

Length:	$35^1/_2$ inches
VSL:	$28^1/_2$ inches
Width, upper bout:	7 inches
Width, waist:	$5^3/_4$ inches
Width, lower bout:	$7^3/_4$ inches
Height of body:	$3^3/_8$ inches

Maurice Matteson's Nathan Hicks Dulcimer:

Length:	$36^1/_2$ inches
VSL:	$28^7/_8$ inches
Width, upper bout:	6 inches
Width, waist:	$4^5/_8$ inches
Width, lower bout:	7 inches
Height of body:	$1^3/_4$ inches

Chapter 5

Margaret Motter's 1929 Jethro Amburgey Dulcimer:

Length:	$32^1/_2$ inches
VSL:	28 inches

Width, upper bout:	4$^1/_4$ inches
Width, waist:	3 inches
Width, lower bout:	5$^3/_4$ inches
Height of body:	1$^5/_8$ inches

Josiah Combs's 1903 Thomas Dulcimer:

Length:	33$^9/_{16}$ inches
VSL:	28 inches
Width, upper bout:	4$^3/_8$ inches
Width, waist:	3$^1/_{16}$ inches
Width, lower bout:	5$^3/_{16}$ inches
Height of body:	1$^3/_{16}$ inches

As is explained in chapter 5, Amburgey based his instruments on patterns provided by Thomas. The variations in the measurements of these two instruments, notably the greater length of the Thomas, reflect the facts that Thomas's own instruments showed variations, and that, in the mountains, "copies" were rarely exact.

Chapter 6

Homer Ledford Dulcimer (photo, page 127):

Length:	34 inches
VSL:	26$^1/_2$ inches
Width, upper bout:	5$^1/_4$ inches
Width, waist:	3$^7/_8$ inches
Width, lower bout:	6$^1/_2$ inches
Height of body:	1$^1/_2$ inches

Clifford Glenn Dulcimer (photo, page 130):

Length:	35$^1/_8$ inches
VSL:	28 inches
Width, upper bout:	5$^1/_2$ inches
Width, waist:	3$^9/_{16}$ inches
Width, lower bout:	6$^1/_2$ inches
Height of body:	1$^1/_2$ inches

Edd Presnell Dulcimer (photo, page 132):

Length:	34$^1/_2$ inches
VSL:	29 inches

Width, upper bout:	$4^5/_8$ inches
Width, waist:	$3^1/_8$ inches
Width, lower bout:	$6^3/_{16}$ inches
Height of body:	$1^7/_8$ inches

Appendix B

Fretting Pattern of the Ache Scheitholt

Old scheitholts and dulcimers were generally fretted by ear. A common method was to move the finger down the fret board, plucking the string, until the interval sounded right. The fret board was marked at that spot, and small holes were drilled to accommodate the staple-style frets. A variant of this method, used by the old-time dulcimer makers Edd Presnell and Homer Ledford, is described in chapter 6. Alternatively, the fret pattern of another instrument was copied, inaccuracies and all.

On many old scheitholts and dulcimers, the maker did not attempt to provide accurate tones and halftones at the upper end of the scale. After about the tenth to twelfth fret in many instruments, the frets revert to approximately equal spacing.

When a dulcimer maker named Bert Berry of Chesapeake, Virginia, read about the Ache scheitholt in my dulcimer history column in the *Dulcimer Players News*, he contacted Jeanette Hamner and asked if he could visit and measure the instrument carefully for the purpose of making a replica. She readily consented.

As part of his measuring task, Bert checked the spacing of the frets and compared it to the correct measurements for the instrument's string span. His measurements reveal a common situation with old scheitholts and dulcimers, that the fretting is inaccurate. The errors, however, are not large. Only frets number 1, 2, 11, and 12 stray about five millimeters or more from fully correct position.

Fret No.	Measured spacing	Correct spacing
1	60 mm	66.81 mm
2	122	126.34
3	152.5	153.63
4	203.5	203.7
5	244	248.31
6	271	268.76
7	305	306.28
8	340.5	339.71
9	366.8	369.49
10	382.5	383.14
11	403.3	408.2
12	425.5	430.52
13	440.5	440.75
14	456.8	459.53

The Mystery of the Scale

We come now to a matter that presents us with a mystery. The "correct spacing" given above is for a standard dulcimer scale for this instrument's vibrating string length (the span of the strings from nut to bridge), which is 24^1/8 inches. As is explained in chapter 1, traditional dulcimers are fretted in such a fashion that, if one depresses the melody string at the third fret and picks it, and then proceeds down the fret board fret by fret to the tenth fret, picking the string at each fret, one will play the major/Ionian scale. We think of it as:

do re mi fa sol la ti do

The major scale has halftones between the third and fourth and between the seventh and eighth tones of the scale. If one begins an eight-note scale at the open string rather than at the third fret, one gets a halftone instead of a whole tone at the seventh note of the scale. The result is:

do re mi fa sol la **ti/flat** do

As is described in chapter 1, one can get this effect by playing a scale from G to G on the piano on the white keys only. Going up to F-sharp at the seventh tone isn't allowed. This scale with a flatted seventh is the scale of the Mixolydian mode. Old-time music lovers will have no trouble identifying some tunes that employ this scale. Think of "Old Joe Clark," "Fire on the Mountain," and "Darling Cory."

Now, suppose you would like your instrument to play the major/Ionian scale from the open string instead of the third fret. Nothing to it. Ti-flat is the only offender in the Mixolydian scale that begins from the open string. To get rid of it, just expand the fretting interval between the fifth and sixth frets from a halftone to a whole tone. This will crowd the next interval down to a halftone, as it is between B and C on the piano. One is then all set. Starting from the open string, one now gets exactly what one is after:

do re mi fa sol la ti do

One encounters a number of old scheitholts, and a few old dulcimers, with fret patterns that have been altered in exactly this fashion. See, for example, the scheitholts that are illustrated in figures 14 and 16 in my book *The Story of the Dulcimer*. The little trick was obviously no secret.

Now, let's look at the Ache scheitholt. Was it Samuel's intention that the major scale should be played from the open string? The answer, as indicated by the letters for the key of C that are stenciled along the fret board, is almost certainly yes. Is the instrument fretted so that it will play the major scale from the open string? The answer is no. The halftone between the sixth and seventh frets has not been expanded to a full tone, and the ensuing interval crowded down to a halftone. If the player uses the stenciled letters as the guide to his scale, he or she will get ti-flat at the seventh tone of his scale. In effect, he or she will be playing in the Mixolydian mode.

Now, did Samuel want his instrument set up to play Mixolydian tunes such as "Old Joe Clark," "Fire on the Mountain," and "Darling Cory," at the virtual sacrifice of its ability to play major tunes? I doubt it.

What is the plot of the tale? Did Samuel have insufficient understanding of the fretting pattern that was known to him through tradition? Or is there something else, something deeper and less accidental, that we no longer know?

Perhaps we could assume that the presence of that pesky ti-flat was just accepted. Old-time dulcimer players were immensely forgiving of tonal irregularities in their scales, and Samuel and his bride might have been the same. And in addition, many old tunes do not employ the seventh tone of the scale at all. Maybe the idea was to avoid tunes that used it.

We could look at it that way. But it's only a guess.

The reader may have a final question. Doesn't it make sense for the major/Ionian scale to start at the open fret? Why does it start at the third fret on the scale of most traditional dulcimers and scheitholts?

The answer, or, rather, answers, reflect some old folk wisdom:

- First, if the major scale starts at the third fret, one can carry tunes down to three notes below do, which is where a lot of them go. Think of "Red River Valley," "My Home's Across the Blue Ridge Mountains," and a hundred others. On an instrument with do at the open fret, one must play such tunes on the second octave. While this is feasible, it is more difficult because the frets are more closely spaced, and the sound is less appealing.
- Second, it turns out that, if the major scale starts at the third fret, it is easier to retune the instrument to play in other musical modes. Ask any dulcimer player.

Appendix C

Winners of the Dulcimer Contest, Old Fiddlers Convention, Galax, Virginia

The following information is taken from the book *The First Forty Years of the Old Fiddlers Convention, Galax, Virginia*, by Herman K. Williams. The book lists the winners of the various contests at the convention from 1935 through 1974 and provides supplementary information.

The following should be noted:

- Two conventions were held in 1935. The convention in April was a trial run. It was so successful that a larger-scale effort was immediately planned for October. It was also successful, and the event was established on an annual basis.
- The records of the October 1935 convention state the contestant's place of residence and the song or tune that the contestant played and/or sang. Records of subsequent conventions provide the place of residence only.
- The records for the 1938 convention have been lost.
- The 1942 convention was shortened to one day because of the wartime restrictions on automobile travel. Only one dulcimer winner was selected in that year. No conventions were held during the war years 1943 and 1944.
- When the convention was resumed in 1945, the dulcimer

contest was dropped. It was not reinstated until 1974, the last year for which the book provides coverage.

A fine early picture of Raymond Melton playing while a number of musicians watch, with the caption, "Showing How to Play Dulcimer: Raymond Melton," appears on page 16 of the book.

A leading Galax-area string band of the 1930s, called the Bogtrotters band, won the string band contest in 1935. A member of this band was a second-generation Galax medical doctor, Dr. W. P. Davis, who played the Autoharp and also secured engagements for the band. An article on the 1935 contest in the October 31, 1935, issue of the *Galax Post Herald* states, "Dr. W. P. Davis conducted the dulcimer and folk song contests, giving an interesting history of the dulcimer, the oldest of the present musical instruments." I would give a lot for a tape of his comments.

Dulcimer Contest Winners

April 1935

Ruth Melton, Galax, Virginia

October 1935

1. Ruth Melton, Galax, Virginia. "Ebenezer."
2. Lina Melton,* Galax, Virginia. "Walkin' in My Sleep."

1936

1. Jacob Melton, Galax, Virginia
2. Lina Melton, Galax, Virginia

1937

1. Raymond Melton, Woodlawn, Virginia
2. Velma Nester (Musser),** Dugspur, Virginia
3. Jacob Melton, Galax, Virginia

---

*The book gives Lina's name incorrectly as Tina Melton at the two starred places in the list.

** Velma's name is incorrectly spelled "Belva" in the list.

1939

1. Raymond Melton, Woodlawn, Virginia
2. Velma Musser, Galax, Virginia
3. Jacob Melton, Galax, Virginia

1940

1. Raymond Melton, Woodlawn, Virginia
2. Lina Melton,* Woodlawn, Virginia

1941

1. Blanch Melton, Woodlawn, Virginia
2. Raymond Melton, Galax, Virginia
3. Jacob Melton, Galax, Virginia

1942

1. Blanch Melton, Woodlawn, Virginia

1974

1. Bonnie Russell, Galax, Virginia
2. Raymond Melton, Woodlawn, Virginia
3. Terry W. Burcham, Huntsville, Alabama
4. Roscoe Russell, Galax, Virginia
5. Velma Musser, Galax, Virginia

In addition to Raymond Melton's placing among the 1974 winners, it is impressive to note that Velma Nester Musser was a winner in 1937, 1939, and 1974. Velma is not related to the Meltons. Several Library of Congress recordings of Velma Musser, made in 1965, are listed at the end of chapter 5.

Appendix D

Newspaper Story on Nineveh Presnell and His Dulcimer

The author's file contains a rather faint Xerox of a newspaper clipping, with a notation stating that it appeared in a Johnson City, Tennessee, newspaper about 1959. The story, which is on Nineveh Presnell and his dulcimer, included a picture of Nineveh sitting on his porch and playing his instrument, which, unfortunately, is much too indistinct in the Xerox copy to reproduce.

The caption accompanying the photograph reads, "WHILES AWAY THE TIME—Passing the time on the front porch of his home, N. V. Presnell, 77-year-old retired farmer of Beech Creek section in Watauga County, N.C., plays his 73-year-old dulcimer."

In addition to its value as a record of Nineveh and his playing, the article reflects the low level of general knowledge of the dulcimer at that time. The reporter does not know the difference between a hammered and an Appalachian dulcimer and is clearly puzzled by what he found in *Webster's International Dictionary.* This confusion led, in the 1970s, to general use of the adjectives "hammered" and "Appalachian" to describe instruments that previously got along without them. The text of the article is as follows:

149

Unusual Instrument . . . Retired Beech Creek Farmer Kills Time Playing Dulcimer

Beech Creek, N.C.—No more beautiful, soothing music can be found than that which comes from the dulcimer, if the player is skilled, and the instrument is a good one.

One such skilled person is N. V. Presnell, a 77-year-old retired farmer of Beech Creek. His instrument is a good one made by his father, the late E. T. Presnell, 73 years ago.

Many Hours

Presnell spends many hours playing his dulcimer at his home—the old home of his father and the house in which he was born. The farm on which the house stands has been in the Presnell family for more than 130 years.

The dulcimer owned by Presnell is the oldest instrument of its kind in this section and is believed to be one of the oldest to be found anywhere.

May Be Similar

What a lot of persons are interested in is whether the instrument used by Presnell and others in the mountainous sections of North Carolina and other areas are similar to the ones referred to in the Bible.

About 600 years before Christ, King Nebuchadnezzar of Babylon set up a great image of gold in the plains of Dura in the province of Babylon. A herald was sent forth to cry aloud to the people: "That at what time ye hear the sound of the cornet, flute, harp, sackbut, psaltery, dulcimer and all kinds of music, ye fall down and worship the golden image that Nebuchadnezzar the king hath set up."

Three Feet Long

The dulcimers used today are about three feet long and made something like a violin. They have three strings. One string is noted by a stick and all three strings picked with a limber splint. The instrument rests on the player's knees.

However, *Webster's International Dictionary* defines the dulcimer

as "an instrument having metallic wires stretched over a trape-
zoidal sound-board with a compass of two or three octaves. It is
played with two light hammers held in hands and from it was
derived the idea of the piano action. Used erroneously to trans-
late the Greek symphonia, now thought to have been a kind of
bagpipe."

No Resemblance

Pictures of the dulcimer described in the dictionary differ from
the one used by Presnell in that it has no resemblance to a violin.
It is flat with the length longer than the width, which is the same
from end to end.

Appendix E

Ordering Dulcimers from Old-Time Makers

Three dulcimer makers who are described in this book, one each from the Virginia, North Carolina, and Kentucky traditions, were making and selling dulcimers as of 1997. This circumstance makes it possible to acquire dulcimers with direct roots in each of the traditions. The price of dulcimers made by all three makers is in the $200 to $300 range. Addresses, phone numbers, and other information are provided below.

Virginia

Jacob Ray Melton
Route 3, Box 183
Galax, Virginia 24333
(703) 236-4543

Jacob Ray and his work are described in chapter 3. Jacob Ray has been experiencing health problems, and his output is small, but he is still making instruments. His dulcimers are purely traditional, with no relation to the folk revival other than the use of modern mechanical tuners instead of tuners cut from old guitar and mandolin plates.

Potential buyers should understand that, with Jacob Ray, they are "buying history." Jacob Ray's instruments are large, simply constructed by the standards of many modern folk-revival dulcimers, and not highly finished. They are usually fretted with wire staples that run under only two of the four strings. The instruments therefore cannot be chorded in modern folk-revival style. All four strings are intended to be tuned to the same note. Two strings are fretted and two play as drones. These instruments produce the true sound of the old Virginia dulcimer, as if the last one hundred years had never been. I believe that anyone with an interest in the history of the dulcimer, should own one of these instruments.

North Carolina

Clifford Glenn
631 Big Branch Road
Sugar Grove, North Carolina 28697
(704) 297-2297

Clifford Glenn and his work are described in chapter 6. Clifford makes fine dulcimers in the traditional North Carolina pattern as descended from Eli Presnell's 1885 dulcimer. They are beautifully crafted, and are available in various woods and combinations of woods. If you want the closest thing to the old tradition, ask for the North Carolina pattern, three strings, without the $6^1/_2$ fret. If your heart is a bit more modern, you can order a four-string instrument with a paired melody string, and/or request a $6^1/_2$ fret and/or request mechanical tuners instead of wooden tuning pegs.

Kentucky

Homer Ledford
125 Sunset Heights
Winchester, Kentucky 40391
(606) 744-3974

Homer Ledford and his work are described in chapter 6. Like Clifford Glenn, Homer Ledford is a superb craftsman who makes a beautiful instrument. As with Clifford, you can order three or four strings, with or without the $6^1/2$ fret. Homer makes many kinds of instruments. To order the traditional pattern based on the old Cumberland dulcimer, ask for his YP-1900 model.

Selected Bibliography

The following books and publications have been especially help-
ful to me in understanding the world of Appalachia and the history of the dulcimer.

*Blue Ridge Folk Instruments and Their Makers: An Exhibit Organized by the
Blue Ridge Institute of Ferrum College, Ferrum, Virginia*. 1992. Excellent
photographs and text. Contact Blue Ridge Institute, Ferrum College,
Ferrum, Virginia 24088, for information on availability and price.

Boone, Hubert. *De hommel in de Lage Landen (The Hommel in the Low Countries)*. Brussels Museum of Musical Instruments Bulletin, Vol. V, 1975.
This unique publication contains scores of photographs of old European fretted zithers and their players, and even includes pictures of
American maker Jethro Amburgey and traditional Tennessee player
Lucy Steele. Incredibly, this item is in print. Contact Frits Knuf Publishers, P.O. Box 720, 4116 ZJ Buren, The Netherlands, ask for their
catalog of Musicology, and check under the listing for the Brussels
Museum of Musical Instruments *Bulletin*.

England, Rhonda George. *Voices From the History of Teaching: Katherine
Pettit, May Stone and Elizabeth Watts at Hindman Settlement School 1899–
1956*. Unpublished Ph.D. thesis, Lexington, Ky: University of Kentucky, 1990. In my opinion, this thesis leaves something to be desired
as a well-argued scholarly work, but it contains lots of fascinating information, including copious selections from the diary of Katherine
Pettit and the correspondence of Elizabeth Watts.

Hicks, John Henry, Mattie and Barnabas B. *The Hicks Families of Western
North Carolina (Watauga River Lines)*. Boone, North Carolina, 1991. John
Henry Hicks spent twenty-five years compiling this 463-page work.
Contact John Henry Hicks, Sugar Grove, North Carolina 28679 for in-
formation on availability and price.

Irwin, John Rice. *Musical Instruments of the Southern Appalachian Mountains*. Norris, Tennessee: Museum of Appalachia Press, 1979. This charming item is subtitled, "A history of the author's collection housed in the Museum of Apppalachia." The book describes and illustrates a number of old dulcimers, and pays as much attention to the owners and players as it does to the instruments. John Rice Irwin, proprietor of this privately owned museum, has been collecting mountain artifacts since the 1960s. In 1989, he received a MacArthur Foundation "genius award," and he and his museum were featured in an article entitled, "Bark Grinders and Fly Minders Tell a Tale of Appalachia," by Jeannie Ralston, in the February 1996 issue of *Smithsonian* magazine.

Isbell, Robert, *The Last Chivaree: The Hicks Family of Beech Mountain*. Chapel Hill, N.C.: University of North Carolina Press, 1996. The great merit of this book is the fully rounded portrait that it provides of mountain life in the years before and shortly after World War II, including its ever-present hardship.

Kincaid, Robert L. *The Wilderness Road*. Indianapolis, Ind.: Bobbs Merrill 1947, reprinted by several other publishers and currently in print. This is the basic work. It doesn't supplant Pusey's book, listed below; nothing could.

Long, Lucy. *The Negotiation of Tradition: Collectors, Community, and the Appalachian Dulcimer in Beech Mountain, North Carolina*. Unpublished Ph.D. thesis, Philadelphia, Pa.: University of Pennsylvania, 1995. Discussed in the text. Fascinating! As for "negotiation" versus "cultural imposition," my preference for Lucy's approach is stated in chapter 5.

Matteson, Maurice. *Beech Mountain Folk-Songs and Ballads, Collected, arranged, and provided with piano accompaniments by Maurice Matteson*. Texts edited and foreword written by Mellinger Edward Henry. Schirmer's American Folk-Song Series, Set 15. New York, N.Y.: G. Schirmer, Inc. (1936). This book is discussed in the text.

Mullins, Mike, Geneva Smith, and Ron Daley. Coeditors, *Knott County, Kentucky History and Families, 1884–1994*. Paducah, Kentucky: Turner Publishing Company, 1985. Invaluable. A little over a thousand copies were printed, all but 100 of which were presold before publication. If you missed it, you missed something wonderful. See if you can borrow it from somewhere on interlibrary loan.

Pusey, William Allen. *The Wilderness Road to Kentucky, Its Location and Features*. New York, N.Y.: George H. Doran Company, 1921. Pusey, a medical doctor, was the great-grandson of William Brown, who traveled the Wilderness Road in 1782 and kept a journal, which has been preserved. In the years 1919 to 1921, Pusey determined the exact location of the Road, which was then not fully known, and published the information in this book with many photographs. The book is wonderful and rare. You will probably pay a good deal for it if you can locate a copy in the second-hand trade, but you should do so with a glad heart. The frontispiece, showing the doctor's old touring car with the top down and a 1920 Virginia license, parked beside the unpaved road in the saddle of Cumberland Gap, is worth the price all by itself.

Raine, James Watt. *The Land of Saddlebags: A Study of the Mountain People of Appalachia*. Published jointly by Council of Women for Home Missions and Missionary Education Movement of the United States and Canada, 1924. Reprinted a number of times. Long out of print but not too hard to find in the second hand trade. Raine was head of the English Department at Berea College. The book, based on years of firsthand observation, is beautifully written. It includes several songs and a photograph of a young man playing a Thomas dulcimer with the same kind of sound holes as the 1891 Thomas described in chapter 5.

Ritchie, Jean. *The Dulcimer Book*. Original edition, New York, N.Y.: Oak Publications 1963, with many reprintings. The first book about the dulcimer, and still fresh and wonderful.

———. *Dulcimer People*. Oak Publishing Company, 1975. Additional information on Jean and on the dulcimer scene as it stood at the time of publication.

Scarborough, Dorothy. *A Song Catcher in the Southern Mountains: American Folk Songs of British Ancestry*. New York, N.Y.: AMS Press, 1966. Original edition, Columbia University Press, 1937. Includes some transcriptions of dulcimer tunes played by Clara Callaghan of Saluda, North Carolina, about 1932. I have some doubts about this material; the tunes and text sound like standard printed British versions. The book is nevertheless charming.

Sharp, Cecil and Maud Karpeles. *English Folk Songs from the Southern Appalachians*. London: Oxford University Press, 1932, republished 1960. These two English folk-song collectors produced one of the greatest of all books about America. Incredibly, it has been out of print for a number of years as of the time of the writing of this book. An article on the 1916 to 1918 collecting trips on which the book was based, entitled "A Man Who Mined Musical Gold in the Southern Hills," by Tony Scherman, appeared in the April 1985 issue of *Smithsonian* magazine.

———. *80 Appalachian Folk Songs, Collected by Cecil Sharp and Maud Karpeles*. Faber & Faber, 1968, reprinted many times. A selection from *English Folk Songs from the Southern Appalachians*. The best you can do while the big book remains out of print.

Smith, L. Allen. *A Catalog of Pre-Revival Appalachian Dulcimers*. Columbia, Mo: University of Missouri Press, 1983. Out of print, and indispensable. The first scholarly work on the dulcimer, and the seedbed of all subsequent work.

Smith, Ralph Lee. *The Story of the Dulcimer*. Cosby, Tn.: Crying Creek Publishers, 1986. My contribution.

Warner, Anne. *Traditional American Folk Songs from the Anne and Frank Warner Collection*. Syracuse, NY: Syracuse University Press, 1984. Wonderful personal recollections of the Hicks family of Western North Carolina, whom the Warners visited in 1938, and careful transcriptions of many songs.

Whisnant, David E. *All That Is Native and Fine: The Politics of Culture in an American Region*. Chapel Hill, N.C.: University of North Carolina Press, 1983. This book is discussed in chapter 5.

Wilgus, D. K. *Anglo-American Folksong Scholarship Since 1898.* Westport, Ct. Greenwood Press, 1982. Original edition, Rutgers University Press, 1959. This was Wilgus's Ph.D. thesis. It contains more about early twentieth century scholarly wrangling over ballads than matters to most people today, but I confess that I enjoyed all of it.

Williams, Herman K. *The First Forty Years of the Old Fiddlers Convention, Galax, Virginia.* n.p., n.d. A highly interesting local production.

Index

Whisnant, David, 95
Wiesner, Jerome, 47
Wilgus, D. K., 87
Williams, Joe, 23
Wiseman, Josie, 17, 27
Women's Christian Temperance
Union, 90

Works Progress Administration
(WPA), 116
Folk Arts Committee, 71
fretted zither with foot pedels.
See Siegrist, Charles C.
Zingsheim, Kay, 23
zither, 13, 22

About the Author

Ralph Lee Smith is a leading authority on the history of the Appalachian dulcimer, and is a performer of traditional American folk music. His book *The Story of the Dulcimer* is the standard history of the instrument. His recordings include *Dulcimer: Old Time and Traditional Music* and *Tunes of the Blue Ridge and Great Smoky Mountains.* He has taught dulcimer classes and seminars at Appalachian State University, the University of Virginia, and the Augusta Heritage Festival at Davis and Elkins College. He is coeditor of the American Folk Music and Musicians Series for Scarecrow Press. Ralph holds a B.A. in English Literature from Swarthmore College and an M.Ed. from the University of Virginia.